CW01646433

TEN NEW CHURCHES

TEN NEW CHURCHES

Edited by

Roger Forster

MARC EUROPE

THE BRITISH CHURCH GROWTH ASSOCIATION

British Library Cataloguing in Publication Data

Ten new churches.
1. Church development, New
2. Church Growth——Great Britain
I. Forster, Roger
254′.00941 BV652.24

ISBN 0-947697-20-9 (MARC)
0-948704-01-2 (BCGA)

The editor is grateful to Marshall Pickering for permission to use extracts of *Let There Be Life* by Andrew Kane, published 1983 in chapter 9 of this book.

MARC Europe is an integral part of World Vision, an international Christian humanitarian organisation. MARC's object is to assist Christian leaders with factual information, surveys, management skills, strategic planning and other tools for evangelism. MARC Europe also publishes and distributes related books on mission, church growth, management, spiritual maturity and other topics.

The British Church Growth Association is a coordinating body for those interested in the growth (spiritual, numerical, organic and incarnational) of the British church today. It comprises researchers, teachers, consultants and practitioners who share information, insights, experience, and new thinking through regional and national activities, a regular journal, occasional publications and other resources, seminars and conferences. It is located at 59 Warrington Road, Harrow, Middlesex HA1 1SZ.

Contents

TEN NEW CHURCHES

1 The Laos Community Dunmurry, Belfast

2 Church of the Redeemer, Shadsworth, Blackburn

3 Ichthus Christian Fellowship, Forest Hill, London

4 Anfield Road Fellowship, Liverpool

5 Tayside Christian Fellowship, Perth

6 Newtown Church, Newtown, Mid Wales

7 Isca Christian Fellowship, Exeter

8 The King's Church, Aldershot

9 New Life Church, Worthing

10 Outpouring Ministries, Bedmond, St Albans

INTRODUCTION

Roger Forster

Roger Forster was converted to Christ as a student at Cambridge University in 1951. He served in the RAF as a National Service Officer, having studied mathematics and theology. He subsequently used the former to teach for a short while, but soon, under increasing demands, began to travel in evangelism and Bible teaching at home and abroad. This he has continued to do for nearly thirty years, serving in many denominations.

For some while he and his wife ran their home as an extended family for the socially maladjusted. He currently leads the fellowship, training programme, and ministry team of the Ichthus Christian Fellowship. He has written two books and co-authored two more.

He has served on the council of the Evangelical Alliance and chaired the EA Committee for Evangelism for many years. It has also been his privilege to serve on many interdenominational bodies including The Consultation on World Evangelism and the Nationwide Initiative on Evangelism. He is the Vice-President of the University and Colleges Christian Fellowship (UCCF).

Variety, vitality, and viability sum up the impressions made by the new churches recorded in the following chapters. In the light of continuing decline in the total membership of the mainline churches in the United Kingdom since 1916 these impressions are remarkable—one might almost say out of character—for the church in general. However they are true and exciting not only for the ten churches presented here but for the hundreds, maybe thousands, of new churches springing up in the land. Such stories augur well for the future. They would seem to say that after all Christianity in the United Kingdom, like Christ its founder, is alive and well.

The churches selected cover a wide geographical area: one is in Scotland, one in Northern Ireland, and one in Wales while the remaining seven are found in England, north, south, south-east and west. The inner city, suburbia, country towns, overspill housing estates, and even a retirement haven, all have stories of new life in Christ. The stories are all different, as are the sorts of people who are finding Christ.

Most, if not all, of the churches whose stories are presented here would be quick to play down their denominational roots or present affiliations. They believe that their success in being born and their continuing service in their respective areas is far more important than their historic associations. Denominational categories break down in the new groupings of Christians. However, even allowing that the multiplicity of movements and streams which exist in Christianity's history together reveal the flow of the Spirit of God, it is startling that in only ten examples of new British churches, the Church of England, Assemblies of God, United Reformed, Baptist, Brethren, and Independents are all found. Those with nominal adherence to Catholicism, those from a wide spread of denominations, and—even more often—those with no denominational adherence at all, find their way on to these pages because of the new life they have found in new churches. You will notice the individual chronicler of each church trying to tell all the colourful testimonies of the many they know who have found Christ, only to be restrained by the limited space each writer was allowed.

God is a God of variety; you will be impressed with the variety of churches found even in so small a number as ten. God is very much alive, full of vitality; that life comes through these ten stories. God knows how to invest himself through Christ into human beings in many ways, so the new churches in Britain today are showing a remarkable capacity for relevance and perseverance in today's world. Neither MARC Europe nor the editor would commit themselves to every view and practice expressed here. However, we do thank God for every one of the ten churches recorded, as answers to many prayers and evidence of the faithfulness of God.

New Churches and Growth

In the midst of this rich diversity certain features emerge which appear to be common to almost all. In identifying and listing these factors—mostly positive—I hope to encourage the birth of more new churches. This is not to produce competition with existing congregations but because there are at least three very serious considerations relating to the emergence of new churches and the advance of the kingdom of God.

First of all, there will soon be many converts on the rising tide of spirituality in this country who will need spiritual homes. This flow of converts has already begun, and pray as we may for labourers as our Lord commanded us (Matthew 9:38), we still find it difficult to keep up with the demand.

Secondly, the lack of Christian teaching among most new converts demands a relevance and style in our church life which many older churches find it hard to produce. These converts (naturally) will only attend and continue in congregations where they are comfortable. Such companies of believers must exist for them. This is not to criticise many existing congregations. It is simply to learn from the obvious, that when babies are brought home the lifestyle of the family has to change to accommodate the babies, not vice versa. The older the parents are, the harder this is.

Grandparents might find the necessary adjustment to a baby's screams and endless nappies virtually impossible.

A church that has lost elasticity in its structures through age-long, undisturbed traditions is to be sympathised with, not condemned; but it must recognise the necessity for younger congregations to do what the older ones must admit to themselves they cannot. Such churches which cannot change must not criticise or denigrate those that can, namely the new, but recognise that they have a different part to play. Of course, if a liniment can be found to lubricate the geriatric condition back into life to offer service to the young Christians, then so be it!

Eddie Gibbs in *Ten Growing Churches* addresses the third consideration when he speaks of encouraging church growth by planting new churches. Congregations spawning new congregations is one of the fastest ways of evangelisation. Many church leaders, from the established Church of England to radicals on the far left, have all expressed themselves in similar terms: that to re-evangelise the United Kingdom one must learn to plant churches again. Inevitably, this means new churches.

Common Factors

With the exception of the first issue discussed below, the common features of new churches are enormously positive. Even among negative possibilities, however, there are solutions.

Opposition

Sometimes the wariness of older neighbouring churches is a problem for the new church. Even when the church is established in its affiliation, as is the Church of the Redeemer, Blackburn, we read of tensions and hints of sheep stealing. Pain and misunderstandings will occur. Sometimes these come from within, sometimes from congregations already functioning for many years nearby. There is no easy answer to this difficulty; however, a few helpful guidelines follow.

Each leader must be sure from God in which context he is called to serve. Elijah had the difficult (more difficult?) task of remaining in the North of Israel to serve the '7,000 who had not bowed the knee to Baal' (1 Kings 19:18). That was not easy when the South was the more 'scriptural' denomination! There they had the temple, sacrifices, priests, Levites, Davidic king, and there they were destined to continue much longer as a movement. Added to this were Elijah's own longing for unity—he built the altar of twelve stones; his desire for obedience—he sacrificed at the time of the evening offering; and his respect for the Davidic dynasty. Like Elijah, many established church leaders are serving in less than ideal conditions. We must know very clearly our own calling from God, and we should honour men and women in their respective callings, even if they are not in 'our stream'.

We must be humble enough to recognise that a large body of thinking exists both in the old and the new churches, which believes church planting is essential to and indeed a necessity for, re-evangelising Britain. We may not agree that this is so but we must accept that those who are planting churches sincerely believe that they are doing it under God. They should not be cheaply criticised as being on ego-trips or wanting to be big fish in small ponds. Those who have planted know the price involved, and there are easier ways of self fulfilment!

It is imperative, as difficult as it may be in practice, that the newly planted churches share their feelings and plans with all the other workers of God in that area. This surely is the rule of love. Love makes itself vulnerable and still goes on loving when hurt, repudiated or rejected.

Although periodic expressions of unity between old and new churches must be arranged and communication kept completely open, it is quite unrealistic to take the position, if you are from an established church, of 'Why don't, or didn't, you all come to my church?' The new would not have come into being if there were not the hunger for something not apparently provided. Most new converts would never feel at home in some older settings.

Ultimately, the faster the church grows in this country, the quicker we will drop the fear of losing our sheep. Proselytism is painful, and losing sheep whom we love to other pastures is sad, yet understandable. However, when there are so many sheep to care for, you do not mind losing some to other shepherds, for it is one flock. Some you might like to lose anyway! More seriously, God said very clearly to me some while ago as our congregations began to spread, '*I* will build my church—*you* seek the Kingdom of God!'

Relationships

At the heart of the matter, the Christian's God is a triad of relationships, Father, Son and Holy Spirit. It is not surprising therefore that Christianity must be experienced at its first and yet profoundest level in relationships, at first with God and then each other. For this Jesus prayed that we should be one as he and the Father, and presumably as he and the Holy Spirit, were one. (John 17:22)

All the new churches express this as one of their fundamental priorities and in so doing seem not only to be touching the heart of the Christian message, but also to be meeting the heart need of humans. Sometimes it is expressed as 'loving one another that the world may know we are Jesus's disciples'. Friendships in Christ are more important than belonging to the same church list. Others emphasise housegroups where life can be nurtured in sharing. All talk of body-life, and some of sitting in circles to see each other, rather than in rows looking at anonymous backs of heads. In so many differing ways new churches are emphasising the need for a loving, caring, sharing life together in Christ. Many lonely and hurt people, let alone those who want wholeness of life in society, seem to find their needs met in this less formal style of relating together as Christians. Acts 4:32—'All the believers were one in heart and mind. No-one claimed that any of his possessions was his own, but they shared everything they had'—is seen to be not an idealistic dream but a practical vision to lay hold of and enjoy in the church in a variety of ways.

Holy Spirit

To walk in line with the Spirit (Galatians 5:25) and to be led by him are also recurring themes. This dependence on the Spirit of God is seen in worship, counselling, guidance and in training workers and leaders. Some describe the immanence of God by his pentecostal Spirit as renewal; others simply state they must be flexible to the way God seems to be indicating that things should be done. Change is here to stay. This style of worship, giving greater freedom for participation by all and for new forms of worship is seen as worshipping in the Spirit. The need in new congregations for maximum involvement requires an emphasis on the Holy Spirit's giving gifts to the ordinary members rather than a dependence on the formally trained seminary man or woman. New Life Church is representative of many others where the changes brought by the Holy Spirit were so radical that although there had been a past history for this congregation, it now qualifies as a new church. The leaders' listening to the Spirit's still small voice, or the prophetic voice being heard (Acts 13:1) are necessities, not additional luxuries. It is clear that the churches in this book represent the vast majority of new companies who are known as charismatic or who tend that way. This raises the third common factor.

Leadership

It is very clear that new churches are guided by new leaders. Perhaps that is too sweeping a statement and could appear to suggest criticism of the leaders of more traditional churches. But let there be no misreading here, for there are outstanding men in well established congregations who are leading their flocks into the end of the twentieth century with great effect and care, having the necessary gifts for the sensitive and delicate changes these congregations have to make. What we mean by 'new leaders', however, is men and women who have the vision necessary to endure the early stages in the birth of a church. Such leadership is invariably corporate, comprised of one or two of these 'visionaries'.

The team ministry that develops has the nature of a body within the Body of Christ which infusses a similar life into the converts, as the Holy Spirit reproduces in them the love and commitment the leaders have amongst each other. This is very different from the traditional one-man-pastor pattern, even though most of the new churches seem to have a *primus inter pares* structure—a chairman amongst equals. 'In the church at Antioch there were prophets and teachers: Barnabas, Simeon called Niger, Lucius of Cyrene, Manaen (who had been brought up with Herod the tetrarch) and Saul.' Acts 13:1 is the pattern of leadership sought after by the new churches in which the prophetic voice is a necessary and important factor in guiding the church.

As well as this visionary leadership there is a common recognition of what used to be called lay-leadership. The participation in decision-making, pastoring, preaching and administration is spread extensively through the new churches, not confined to the trained professionals. The results of this kind of leadership are seen in the rich variety of activities and projects many new churches engage in.

Relevance

For a new church to come into being there must exist a need. Sometimes this could be born of a desire for 'deeper teaching' or 'particular experiences' which produce merely a holy huddle: hardly a church destined by Christ to be sent into the world as an extension of his mission—'As You sent me into the world, I have sent them into the world' (John 17:18). None of the new churches recorded here falls into this snare. Their existence seems more to do with relevance to the outsiders' needs. In Anfield, for example, we see church life as virtually essential for out-of-work youngsters. In most of the churches the worship is lively and relevant, not at all boring or overly pious. New music and songs, easily remembered, are used; any instruments available are incorporated into the joy of celebration. Healings from inner hurts and deliverance from evil supernatural powers immediately meet current national needs, as do love and value for people expressed in social action. These new churches have fewer inhibitions when confronted with a new need and consequently seem often to be touching people where they most readily respond. Perhaps this is why . . .

Social Action

. . . Social action is often high on the agenda. Most of the new churches mention their concern to relate to the disadvantaged and deprived. Schemes for the out-of-work function in the inner city churches such as in Anfield, Liverpool and at Ichthus in London. Youngsters hooked on glue sniffing or drugs are more easily reached when a friend has been delivered through a group of Christians who believe that God's power is at work in their midst. Perhaps this expectation is high in a new church since faith and God's presence were essential for its coming into being and its continuance, whereas in a well established scene, faith may not have been challenged deeply.

There is an obvious advantage in meeting in a community centre, a school, or a room in a public house. People with no church background, the unemployed, the drop-outs or drug abusers can all find their way in and perhaps sit informally, feeling at home more readily than where smart dress and formal buildings, foreign to their culture, are encountered.

Strawberry Plants

Planting more churches seems to be the habit into which most new churches fall. Alan Vincent tells us of his strawberry plants shooting off into the nearby towns. Isca in Exeter now has four congregations and relationships with other new churches which have come into being through their vision and work. Indeed most of our ten will explain how they want and are able to reproduce. The body-life begun and developed in the new church becomes the womb that reproduces similar life.

A new life, a new group, grows as people already in relationships move into the new area as infant bodies while still being supported by the parent body. In other words, it is not an individual alone planting a new work, nor indeed is it a few individuals trying to 'make a church together'. It is rather that those who have lived, shared, loved, and grown together in the parent body now continue in a new location. Already the life of Christ is shown in them and in the community to be evangelised and served.

The first church at Jerusalem serves as such a model. For five or six years it matured under the 'apostles' teaching (Acts 2:42). People even appear to have moved from Galilee and elsewhere to be in the massive Jerusalem church. We could speculate that perhaps 30,000 or more were now believers enjoying life together, having all things in common. New young apostles like Stephen were beginning to come forward. Perhaps God intended a voluntary break-up and dispersion; maybe persecution was part of the plan. In any case, when the persecution began, almost overnight, churches appeared in every town and village of Judea and Galilee, and Samaria was not far behind (Acts 6:8–9:31).

As we seek God's kingdom and many press into it, let us trust and be happy that Christ will direct the sheep into the appropriate pastures for them. He is building his Church, not ours, for the glory of God and for the well-being of humanity.

Chapter 1

The Laos Community

1975

Ken Brown

Robert Mearns, Ken Brown and Sammy Douglas are the leaders of Laos Community Church in Dunmurry, just outside Belfast. This church, consisting now of a congregation of 150, has grown fourfold since 1980. It serves a suburban district of middle class and council homes where there is no main source of employment.

Sammy, married to Gillian, has three children. He and Robert, both full-time in the church, enjoy soccer and keeping tropical fish. Robert and Iris have three children, while Ken and Liz have five. Ken enjoys collecting lead soldiers and gardening; he teaches at the Queen's University in Belfast and is the writer of this chapter.

Sunday in Belfast. The city's large church-going population is almost the only group on the move. Catholics flock to Mass; Salvationists trumpet their way to the citadel; a hundred and one other Protestant denominations assemble in cathedrals, gospel halls, and almost everything in between.

In Dunmurry, a small south Belfast suburb which has retained many of its old village characteristics, the Mearns' green car noses out of a side street to make the short journey to the local hotel where the Laos Community holds its weekly meeting. The family wave at the Browns, occupants of another car approaching from the other side of the village.

The two cars form a small convoy, and others join in. There is an old but trusty Ford containing the church's third elder, a former commander in the Protestant terrorist group, the Ulster Defence Association. From the back grin the Murphys, a Catholic family originally from Dublin. Four boisterous young men roar past in an even older Ford, tactfully slowing as they pull into the car park behind the family of an off-duty policeman. Another car spills out a motley assortment of tattooed men who look as if they might be more at ease carrying crowbars than Bibles.

Gerry, reared in Republican Londonderry, staggers into the hall under a tangle of microphones, wires, and recording equipment. His wife, a Belfast Protestant, settles their two children down in a corner. Paddy Murphy busies himself organising some of the church's numerous unemployed men into a work rota for the following week. Billy, who works in a local bakery, chats with Stephen, halfway through his first tiring year as a houseman in a hospital outside Belfast. Fiona, who hopes to go up to Oxford, inquires after the health of Granny Mcleod, almost 80 and just back from Canada.

By 11.20—in true Irish fashion well after the appointed starting time—the meeting begins. It is a noisy affair in general. Over and above the melodies provided by an assortment of guitars, violins, recorders, bongo drums, a clarinet and a small organ, there is a persistent buzz of sound from the hordes of small children present, for this is predominantly a young church. Sometimes the youngest go out, especially if a long sermon is being preached or if there is a visiting speaker. More usually they remain, absorbed or otherwise in the spontaneous singing, dancing, prophecy, testimony and prayer which go to make up a typical meeting. They share in the breaking of bread when that is the focus of a morning's service. Some of the older ones join quite freely in prayer for the sick and troubled.

In the midst of the constant movement and noise there is an order and purpose as the Spirit moves, now on one, now on another. Above all, there is an overwhelming sense of family, epitomised perhaps by the custom of moving, when appropriate, from a final song of praise into a chorus of 'happy birthday'! Afterwards it is home to late lunches or perhaps, in the summer, a picnic or a football match in the park. Surveying this heterogeneous body of people as they stream out after the meeting, one can but wonder how they came together sharing their lives and living out, in the midst of a bitterly divided province, the truth that in Christ there are no barriers of age, class, or sect that cannot be bridged.

Beginnings

We go back to June 1966. In Belfast's Shankill Road, Robert Mearns, steeped in Orangeism and Protestantism, was 'arrested by God', as he now describes it. With a gang of other youngsters he was walking along the Shankill Road when an old woman unexpectedly confronted him. 'Would you not give your life to God?' she asked, pleading with him over and over again. Later he had time to think about her question. That night when he went home, this time alone, he gave his life to God.

In a city where evangelical preaching was—and is—the norm, and backsliding equally common, his numerous brothers took bets on how long the conversion would last. The most optimistic gave him a fortnight but were surprised when he no longer fought or used bad language.

Meanwhile, on the very same day but on the other side of the Atlantic, an English university student was having his own encounter with God at a gospel service in a seedy area of Toronto. Three years passed before in the purposes of God the paths of these two unlikely church builders started to merge.

In 1969 the Englishman, Ken Brown, went with his newly acquired wife, Liz, to a lecturing post at the Queen's University of Belfast. Among the final year students on his British history course was Robert Mearns who, as leader of a subgroup of the university Christian Union, was praying for a place where his group could meet. The Browns offered their flat close to the university. But how, Robert wondered with some trepidation, could he share with his lecturer his experience of baptism in the Spirit and speaking in tongues? In fact his fears proved groundless, for the Browns had had a similar experience during their years at university in Canterbury.

Yet this common blessing by no means endeared the two men to each other. Living with the Browns as he prepared for his final exams, Robert was surprised to see Ken sharing the cooking and housework, tasks which in the working class culture of the Shankill Road were considered to be fit only for women. For his part Ken, quieter and from a middle class background, did not cope well with the rather rough, extrovert and garrulous Ulsterman who preached at every opportunity—frequently at him! Nor did he accept very graciously some very obvious overtures of friendship. Certainly they could share a prayer meeting or Bible study, but the Englishman's private affairs, like his home, were his castle, and he tended to resent the invasion of either.

This was a time when there was a charismatic renewal among the students at Queen's, a time when future Christian leaders were discovering what God intended for them. A small group, mainly of medical students and nurses, began to meet mid-week in the university area under the general supervision of a local evangelist and with Robert and Ken as two of the main participants. This group continued after Robert, having felt directed to turn down a place at the Asbury Theological Seminary in America, began work at the Goodyear Company, and after Ken and Liz moved out to Dunmurry in order to have more suitable accommodation for their first child. Robert and his new bride, Iris, followed them a couple of months later.

This group hardly seemed likely to develop into anything of significance. All of its members attended different churches on Sundays. Students disappeared during vacations and no-one saw the group as anything more than a midweek spiritual refuge. True, there was honest discussion of problems, fervent prayer and sound teaching but there was no real structure, no acknowledged authority, no discipline, and no underlying commitment.

Yet, prophetically as it turned out, the group did act as a magnet for human casualties—people with deep needs (or sometimes just malingerers) and with whom neither Robert nor Ken felt adequately equipped to deal other than by exercising faith in prayer. Although this often produced results and was faith-building, both men began to feel the need for something more permanent, a vision which the evangelist did not then share. Both were equally frustrated by the lack of freedom and evident sterility of much orthodox church life—at least, the bits they had encountered.

A Cry from the Heart

In the early hours of one morning, after yet another of what were becoming longer and more frequent counselling sessions, the two sat in Robert's car, praying that God would send them some different people with whom they could build on a longer-term basis. 'You know, Lord, ordinary folk, not chronically ill ones, or hypochondriacs, or compulsive liars, just a few normal ones, Lord!' That was a prayer that God began to answer! Another couple emerged to take over the original group and Ken and Robert felt a distinct call from God to begin meeting on Sundays.

They met initially in Ken's house, partly because it was

larger, partly because it had carpet! At the beginning God gave them a vision of a clay-bound garden and indicated that fruitfulness would be the product only of a long, hard slog. So it proved. A few people joined with them on Sundays, and some came to a weekly evening meeting. One or two stayed, others drifted elsewhere. Numbers remained small and there was little apparent sign of much happening.

But all the time God was at work on the fundamental relationship which was to be foundational in what he wanted to build. God had shown quite clearly in another vision that he was knotting together the strands of individual lives to form an effective net for catching others, since by themselves separate strands could catch nothing. Ken was looking for a move. By the mid-1970s the Ulster troubles were at their height. He had, he reckoned, done his bit as a missionary and Ulster was no place for his rapidly increasing family, even though, like Robert, he had quite clearly experienced God's protection in dangerous situations.

In any case, he was ambitious and there was the tempting prospect of a job in Canada. Also he wanted a larger house. One night, unable to sleep, he got up and prayed about the future, asking God specifically for a bigger house as a sign that he was to stay in Belfast. Two days later, Liz chanced upon a small, insignificant advertisement in the local paper. It was for a house which appeared ideal for their needs. A few weeks later, the house was theirs, and the Canadian job rejected. Shortly afterwards, Ken received an unexpected and substantial promotion at the university.

The decision to stay in Belfast created in Robert a much greater sense of security. Gradually, too, his tremendous openness, which belied his sensitive and easily hurt personality, was building a stronger bridge with Ken. This enabled the two men to discuss their differences and views much more openly without either man feeling threatened or rejected.

In 1981 there came a second, and much more strategic

decision, this time on Robert's part. Ever since his conversion he had known that one day he would leave his secular employment to work full time in the ministry. In the Authorised Version of the Bible the verses of commission which the Lord had given to him were underlined and dated. 'Though the vision . . . tarry, wait for it, because it will surely come . . .' (Habakkuk 2:3) proved remarkably accurate; for it was 15 years after his conversion that Robert gave up his job.

With a great deal of encouragement from David Matthews, leader of the Belfast Christian Family, and Norman Barnes from Chadwell Heath, both of whom had for some years been helping the small Dunmurry group, the decision was made. At the weekly meeting, the 20 or so people present agreed that by tithing their incomes they could provide a salary for Robert, albeit smaller than the one he was earning as a middle manager in the electricity service.

It was a momentous step, one which could only be taken when the fundamental relationships were firmly established and when Robert's wife was confident enough to trust herself and her three children to the idea. Once again, the Lord indicated his approval with a blessing, as Iris finally found healing for a condition which had attacked her spasmodically for almost four years.

Some of Robert's acquaintances were surprised when he announced his decision to leave work. Others merely wondered how he was going to fill in his time looking after such a small group of people. Nor did the adjustment to a life without the routine imposed by having regular work prove particularly easy for Robert or his wife. It was again a time of learning and adjustment, but before long the church began to grow.

At one meeting God moved the people to link hands in a circle. There then came a 'word of prophecy' that after the time of being built together as a closely knit family, it was now time to turn, to look outwards, and to welcome others into the kingdom of God. It came as no surprise, therefore, that in each of the first two years of Robert's ministry he prayed for, and saw, a doubling of numbers, though the emphasis of the teaching was always on the quality of life within both the church and the individual, rather than on the size of the membership.

Continuing to Grow

By 1985 the church had about 70 children and 80 committed adults, with more attending the Sunday meeting or one of the smaller weekly groups without formally being in membership. A few of the newcomers came from other similar fellowships for reasons of marriage or geography. A few more left institutional churches in order to join, although as a matter of courtesy every single one was sent back to explain his or her decisions to their previous minister.

One or two were directed to us by the Lord in very specific ways. The Murphys came in response to a vision they had had while working in the Christian Renewal Centre at Rostrevor, near Newry. Another couple felt led to leave a very prosperous lifestyle in Australia on a word from God, and they turned up one Sunday morning and heard the very same word spoken in prophecy as a confirmation of their placement. But the vast majority of the people whom God has added have been from no committed church background at all.

The mechanisms by which growth occurred were varied but the growth owed almost nothing to systematic campaigning, although this may prove to be an option in the future. Most of it came about through individual contacts. Some were drawn in through a weekly morning meeting for wives and toddlers, which Liz Brown helped to initiate. Others were touched by the innate evangelistic gift of particular individuals. One young man, who began meeting with us when he was only 14 was once told prophetically that he would be a channel for many of his peers. Certainly his commitment and enthusiasm for what the Lord was doing resulted in a number of his school friends joining the church. One family, the Douglasses, revealed a gift of generous hospitality and have brought a number of unsaved people to the Lord, mainly from working-class areas of the inner city where they themselves originated.

Cell groups also proved to be effective meeting points. For some years the church members have been organised into a number of small groups, each of which has been largely left to pursue its own activities at a weekly meeting under the guidance of a small team of leaders. Both the leadership and the members have been periodically shuffled around in order to prevent the development of cliques or complacency. It is in these sharing groups, based in essence on Wesley's concept of the class meeting, that much of the basic counselling and teaching has been done. But they have also provided an informal and friendly atmosphere into which newcomers have been easily integrated. Some groups have undertaken more active programmes of outreach.

Underpinning this growth has been, firstly, a great deal of prayer. Members of the church have been encouraged to meet weekly with one or two others with whom they can share their joys or sorrows and also pray for each other, or for individuals and situations involved in the life of the church. The women proved particularly responsive to this, although more recently some of the men have begun to meet in early morning prayer cells. So, too, have a number of the young teenage boys. Occasionally, the committed people in the fellowship are called to a week of prayer and fasting for the specific purpose of seeking God's mind for church development and activity over the succeeding period. All regular group activities are then suspended for a week and replaced by nightly prayer meetings.

Secondly, church teaching has been directed towards encouraging faith and expectation of growth, on the principle that unless there is commitment to and vision for expansion, it will not happen. This has been emphasised in the ministry and prophecy given at a couple of residential weekends organised partly as holiday, and partly to provide a greater sense of call to corporate life and service. Neither the times of prayer and fasting nor the residential weekends have been seen as permanent fixtures in the church calendar but have been arranged, we believe, in accordance with the leading of the Holy Spirit. They will be repeated only as and when God so ordains.

Much of our original discontent with the institutional church in Ulster was caused by its apparent inflexibility and willingness to act only in accordance with custom and precedent. We have tried hard to guard against this same paralysis, though it is striking how quickly forms and approaches become fixed.

Finally, at the heart of the church's expansion has been a wonderful work of grace and patience on God's part in knitting together the two foundational men until they now have a friendship that neither time nor distance can destroy. Furthermore, the relationship of two such diverse individuals has been an expression of the character of the church as described by Paul in Galatians—neither Jew nor Greek, slave nor free, male nor female.

Some Difficulties

Such rapid growth created practical problems which placed considerable pressure on the two church elders. For a long time an adequate meeting hall was foremost in our praying, once numbers grew uncomfortably large for someone's domestic front room. Reluctant to tie up large sums of money in bricks and mortar, we were keen to rent. But local churches were understandably unwilling to make their halls available on Sundays, and the village suffered from a lack of other large meeting places. For a brief spell, we used a local hotel, although we had to meet on Saturdays because the hotel was not open on Sundays.

Three years ago the Lord led us to a wooden and rather scruffy British Legion Hall in an adjacent suburb and this we were able to hire on a rather more permanent basis. By 1984, however, space was again at a premium and the number of people attending exceeded the number of available chairs. The prospect of having to stand throughout the meeting did little to improve punctuality! In 1984, therefore we again made a new hall a priority in our week of prayer and fasting. As we reached the end of the 12 months and prepared for another similar week, so God provided in a most unexpected way. The hotel which we had formerly used on Saturdays agreed to rent us its disco room on Sundays. Its name? 'Lord's Nitespot'!

The growth in numbers further exposed deficiencies in our worship of which we were well aware. Clearly, we could no longer depend upon the services of one lone guitarist. It was with some anxiety that we had to stop him playing anyway as it became apparent that in his heart he had turned away from God. But in response to prayer and our determination to ensure that as far as we knew our praise offering was sincere, God brought to us a number of highly talented musicians. Not least among these were a number of our own children whose involvement in the music has integrated them more comprehensively into church life.

Problems of finance also appeared, as the support of full-time leaders (a second one began work in January 1984), the renting of halls, and the provision of the necessary technical equipment made heavy demands on what is, in the main, a working-class church containing a high proportion of unemployed, low-income earners, and students. Those committed to the fellowship, even the children, were taught the principle of tithing. Although it was not made at all mandatory we believe that a man's attitude to his money indicates accurately the state of his relationship with the Lord.

Sadly, a few folk left us over this issue. Yet for those who have faithfully tithed, even those who had severe debt problems when they joined us, God has provided in unexpected ways and drawn them gradually into relative prosperity. In 1984 the church was able to give away 15 per cent of its income to support outside ministries, as well as raising occasional collections for specific needs. It is in this same spirit of God-inspired generosity that furniture, clothing, cash and cars are freely shared around among the church members.

The paramount need, however, was for people who could share the pastoral burden which became too much for two men and their wives to bear alone. It was not only a matter of sheer numbers but also a product of the fact that God was again directing towards us people who had deep-seated spiritual needs, and who also often suffered from fundamental social problems such as drug addiction, debt, inadequate housing or unstable family relationships. Now we saw the value of that early training. Now we understood why God had caused us to concentrate so much on encouraging healthy family life.

Practical and Spiritual Ministries

Our reputation as a community particularly burdened for the poor and socially deprived began to increase. Amongst the most needy was a group of former prisoners, most of them paramilitaries. One had found the Lord in prison but the rest were drawn in through personal contacts and converted, several at a residential weekend for men. For such as these the process of rehabilitation to society had to be coupled with the task of bringing their whole lifestyle into line with the demands of their new-found faith.

The Lord directed us to rent two houses where such people could live alongside some of the fellowship's single men who were given some pastoral responsibility for them. The bulk of their care, however, was undertaken by a man who was himself once heavily involved in terrorist organisations. At the beginning of 1984 he was appointed the third church elder, given a salary and some freedom to exercise his considerable evangelistic and pastoral gifts.

Alongside the elders God has since raised up half a dozen men who lead the cell groups, take on most of the pastoral work and some of the day-to-day running of church activity. Increasingly they have earned the right to take initatives in worship, teaching, and outreach. Ken has retained overall responsibility for directing the church and organising it.

Robert, although supported still by the church, has started to travel more widely as God has brought him into a fuller and more powerful healing and restoring ministry for those afflicted with sickness, oppressed by evil spirits or suffering from emotional disorders. Opportunities opened up in Dublin, various English cities, Scotland and, more recently, America and Africa. This ministry really began to develop after the 1984 visit to Belfast of Derek Prince, an articulate spokesman of the charismatic movement. It was significant, too, in view of Robert's increased absences, that several of the church's other leaders also experienced God's power in a way which greatly increased the degree of discernment, wisdom, and other spiritual gifts evident in the meetings.

The release of this power was the answer to a prayer which Robert and Ken had often prayed. Given that the gospel was preached in word from virtually every street corner and hoarding in Belfast, they had both longed to see it substantiated by signs. Yet it was many years before an answer was apparent and while there were many issues in church life to which God responded very quickly, there were others which he used to teach his people patience. It was over a year, for example, before we found an adequate hall. A much longer period of prayer elapsed before Iris Mearns was healed. Another couple, who lived on the far side of the city, prayed for nearly three years before they finally got a house near enough to enable them to participate fully in the church.

There are still some folk who remain unhealed, despite

repeated prayers and anointings. In these long battles faith has sometimes grown pretty feeble. There have been other disappointments, too. People have left us with issues unresolved; there have been meetings devoid of life; resentments have sometimes lain too long unconfessed; individuals have failed to mature as we would have wished; children have sometimes proved unresponsive to their parents' commitment and faith. Others have deceived us or taken advantage of us. We have failed to make much meaningful contact with other churches in the village, although we did share for a time with Methodists and Presbyterians in a joint praise service. With some notable exceptions ministers from the institutional church have been suspicious of us, and in a province where there is much religious conservatism there has been considerable corporate and individual distrust of a group which contains people from both Catholic and Protestant traditions and calls both 'Christian'.

Yet we have not, of course, existed entirely in a vacuum. At the individual level many friendships have been formed which easily transcend denominational barriers. For many years, probably, few people in the village knew of our existence, except perhaps neighbours who had to put up with the sound of singing through their party walls! Yet we believed that God was working on that basic relationship, teaching us and preparing us for a day when we would be more publicly seen. In 1984 we sold six hundred tickets for a stage presentation, 'Blowing in the Wind', a revue designed to ask basic questions about the purpose of man's existence. Later in the same year a group of young people formed a choir and sang in the main village street. There was no overt preaching; they sang for the sheer joy of it.

A number of important outside connections have been formed with other similar groups in and around the Belfast area, several of them led by men who were students at the university in the 1970s. There is a monthly meeting of the elders for fellowship, reviewing the activities of each church, and sponsoring joint meetings. There has also been some beneficial exchange of ministry and, as a relatively poor community, we have benefited quite often from the generous giving of our brothers and sisters.

Their recognition of our particular ministry to the poor has encouraged our vision for planting new groups in the inner-city areas and in working-class suburban estates. There is a growing and genuine sense of mutual appreciation, an awareness that God will command a blessing on our divided city when church leaders move together in unity. Nowhere was this better demonstrated than when Derek Prince visited the city in 1984. Almost 2,000 people packed into the final meeting and there was an unprecedented release of healing and deliverance. People turned from their involvement in witchcraft; others were healed of bodily, mental and emotional illness. As one of the elders then put it, in Belfast 'the tide of God is on the turn and coming in.'

Chapter 2

Church of the Redeemer, Shadsworth

1975

Geoff Pearson

The Church of the Redeemer, an Anglican church, serves the parish of Shadsworth in Lancashire. Located on the south-west side of Blackburn amid post-war council estates and more recent deck-access and multi-storey flats, Church of the Redeemer has more than doubled its congregation in the past five years. The Reverend Geoff Pearson, a Liverpudlian with an inevitable enthusiasm for Liverpool Football Club and a passion for the writings of George MacDonald, served the parish from 1977 until March 1985, first as curate in charge and then as vicar.

Geoff and his wife Jean have three children. The Pearsons left Church of the Redeemer when Geoff became Assistant Home Secretary to the Board for Mission and Unity, General Synod of the Church of England.

How should a church cope with a new building development of three multi-storey blocks of flats, and a maze of deck-access flats, on the edge of a large parish?

A new residential area had been created which had no obvious natural proximity to any church, and certainly not to Christ Church, Blackburn, in whose parish it was situated. The new flats were sandwiched between a park and Shadsworth Council Estate. The people would not go to the church, so the church had to go to the people!

The Rev Stanley Fell, vicar of Christ Church, began negotiations with the local authority and was eventually offered the tenancy of a supermarket, shortly to be vacated. The newly-arrived curate, Eddie, and his wife, Rizpah, started services there in August 1969, after a long haul of door-to-door visiting. A steady group of older ladies came from the multi-storey flats, including Jenny, who was an extremely nervous woman. She had lived for years in extraordinarily difficult circumstances; she had lost several children tragically and had marital problems. She was converted, and when her doctor met her later in the street, he saw the difference and asked her what had happened. She told him about the Lord she had encountered, and how he had completely changed her life.

The Parochial Church Council at Christ Church started looking for a permanent building for the embryonic new church, though this initiative was set back by the discovery of dry rot in the main roof of the parish church, which then had to be demolished. The people of Christ Church moved into the parish rooms across the road and kept before them the vision to fulfil an obvious need on the edge of the parish.

Then a site in the corner of a field was offered for the small 'supermarket' fellowship, with the added prospect of over 500 homes to be built in the same area. The proposed position was quite strategic; a community centre was situated across the road, the flats were within a stone's throw, and the new building would be on the edge of the biggest council estate then in existence in Blackburn.

There was a snag. That council estate was part of a neighbouring parish which—under the Anglican system—made work in that area a sensitive question. But with the help and encouragement of the diocesan authorities, the site was purchased and the future looked bright.

Within weeks, however, the local authority then shelved its plans for the houses through economic stringency. At this point a historical precedent was recalled: another daughter church of Christ Church had been built in the fields in 1901, and was now surrounded by houses. Plans for God's building were not shelved, and in December 1975 the Church of the Redeemer, Shadsworth, was dedicated.

Looking a bit like a Mormon church and having a slightly non-Anglican name caused a few confusions. In time, as people came to worship from a whole range of denominational backgrounds, the ambiguity of the building became a strength rather than a weakness.

Terry Pye and his wife Gay, assisting Stanley Fell, had moved into the deck-access flats and were in charge of the new church's life in Shadsworth, for the first 12 months. The building, largely funded by the people of Christ Church, had cost a sacrificial £33,000, and now there was no money left for interior furnishings. Notice boards, lecterns, and heavy wooden pews arrived from other local churches. A large, imposing brass eagle nicknamed Percy, was flown in and looked truly incongruous. (Much later, it took several men to help him fly out.)

The only advantage was that the furniture which made the modern building so inflexible had the hidden benefit of establishing the priority of worship. There was not much else you could do! Terry introduced family services and Gay began to help some young women to experience the joy and reality of knowing Jesus. Before leaving in 1977 to go to Korea with the Overseas Missionary Fellowship, Terry and Gay left the nucleus of a missionary-hearted fellowship including an older group of faithful, praying women keen to do God's will.

That same year, Stanley Fell appointed Pat Westall as a parish worker. Previously she had enjoyed an itinerant ministry, and many of her contacts were maintained as she travelled to other churches in Lancashire and Cumbria. Wherever she went she asked groups to pray for this young church in the corner of a field. At first she felt that the church building was like an empty barn: she prayed constantly for the Lord to add to our numbers, and indeed was regularly woken up in the night for this particular ministry of intercession. Probably more things were brought about at the Redeemer through the prayers of Pat Westall than through anything else. She was no plaster saint, but had a joy and zest for life—she loved thrillers, had a passion for fish and chips, and always enjoyed her holidays to the utmost. When Pat prayed in public we were lifted to the very presence of God and seemed to be listening to a very special intimate conversation. Her prayers, as well as those of many others whom she encouraged to use this gift, were the backbone for all the evangelistic projects and new strategies that were undertaken. When she died of cancer in January 1983 letters flooded in from all over the world as those who knew her shared their sense of loss.

Establishing the New Church

The church now needed some stability in its leadership. I was appointed curate-in-charge in 1977 and stayed for eight years. For the first six, my family and I lived in a council house on the estate. Living in this way amongst our people, and the personal style of ministry (as Terry and Gay had already found in the flats) was costly but vital. A smart new vicarage set back from the road can easily distance the leadership from the people whom the church is there to serve.

The vicar's willingness to allow responsibility for the new church to rest in hands other than his own allowed the new congregation great freedom, and, unfettered by rigid adherence to familiar traditions, the church easily and naturally assumed a form of worship that reflected (usually!) both joy and spontaneity. What we wanted was to be able to sing to God rather than simply about him, to be free to worship in choruses as well as hymns, with greater congregational participation, allowance for open prayer, and for ministry through the gifts of the Holy Spirit.

In developing its own pattern of authority, planning and decision making, the path was less easy. The Redeemer fellowship held church business meetings three times a year, but as a daughter church, its representatives served on the Parochial Church Council of Christ Church, and the daughter was by no means a smaller version of the mother. Tensions were inevitable and the presence of a new church in its first flush of enthusiasm and experience of blessing called for some adjustment from the rest of the PCC, while the new fellowship needed to avoid bearing resentment from the frustration of feeling held back, or misunderstood. Over the years the gap naturally widened until the daughter left home; only then were the tensions really resolved.

Besides its ordained man and parish worker, the church had the support of two dedicated church-wardens and two young couples from Christ Church. Their physical and prayerful support in the first 12 months kept the vision alive. In a needy area any church is likely to have a crisis-centred ministry, and Shadsworth was no exception. However, a main priority was always to build up the body of Christ in order that, together, the people might reach out more effectively through the power of God to unbelievers. Thus we had two parallel, on-going aims: to grow in numbers and also in spiritual depth. It was not until the church had built up a strong base that it could begin to minister fully to the many needy people in the area, especially—as was soon the case—to the young glue-sniffers in local estates.

The evangelistic work flourished through personal invitation. New Christians who were full of enthusiasm for the Lord were able to invite friends, workmates, relations to a meeting of people who were friendly, and to worship that was warm and alive. A monthly contact meeting in the evenings existed to forge links with young women; it provided a relaxed setting for friendly discussion. A fortnightly ladies' fellowship run by Pat served the needs of older women; it provided an opportunity for corporate prayer and for the establishment of links with other neighbouring churches. A mums-and-babies' club was begun in the Shadsworth Community Centre across the road—neutral territory that helped people cross the threshold of a church organisation; through the warmth of friendship and testimony, several young mothers were helped to a living faith. On Sunday mornings, a crèche for babies and Sunday School for the children (all held in the community centre as the church had no extra rooms), meant whole families were catered for, and often whole familes came—fathers as well as mothers and children.

There were plenty of occasions for special efforts. A home mission team from 'The Come back to God Campaign', now based in Scotland, was just right for our area and conducted four full-scale missions over a period of five years. They helped people in a disadvantaged area to have a greater sense of self-worth and deeper expectations. We had a season of evangelistic films and we experimented with gospel concerts. Both quickened the life of the church and added a few to our numbers as well as reaching some who would never otherwise have had contact with us.

There were some classic failures; one youth outreach was even helped by the rock group's use of smoke bombs, which conveniently hid the absence of young people in the audience. That failure, however, encouraged us to review our strategy among young people and to go out to where the young people were: a secular youth club, and the alleys where glue-sniffing was becoming a growing menace. The eventual outcome was that two men from the church started going out at night to meet youngsters. One young man, Tim, gave up his plumbing business and started full-time youth work in the area, largely supported by Christian sponsors.

Other challenges were facing us in an institutional guise with a large hospital and four state schools nearby. These made us aware of the mission field constantly around us. As a way of beginning to minister to our environment, therefore, we had a series of special HOPE services—Hear Our Personal Experience.

Each year, to, we had a week's parish holiday and a Sunday school camp; these took a lot of effort but were always worthwhile in forging and deepening relationships. Constantly, we learned to be surprised. God honoured our evangelistic intentions although—more often than not—people were added to the church in his own sovereign way, rather than according to our strategic planning.

Structures

One of the real advantages of a new church is the lack of any handicapping traditions. It is surprising how quickly today's freedoms become tomorrow's bondages, but at least you are forced to think about what you start and why, and can encourage a constant review. There is a real temptation to want structures similar to an 'established' set-up overnight, but this is a temptation to be resisted.

There was obvious need of organisation in the children's work. The Sunday school was developing slowly, but we noticed that children of church families were regularly missing because of parade services elsewhere. To attract children from the estate, with no church links some new structure was needed. We looked at the various organisations available, and decided that the Campaigner uniformed organisation was the right one for our church. We were impressed with its links with the local churches, its biblical base and godly leaders who went out of their way to help us get started. A neighbouring Anglican church had a large clan, and their leaders gave tremendous help and support through the difficult early days.

The decision to have Campaigners was an act of faith in view of the amount of leadership for which such a movement calls. Few people were professional leaders or had shown obvious natural leadership, so we had no alternative but to place young, inexperienced Christians in a position of authority and pastoral responsibility. It was a risk but on the whole this worked, although the challenge of absorbing all the Campaigner material and facing the children with confidence left little energy for working at relationships among the Campaigner leaders. Some painful learning consumed a lot of time and served to emphasise again and again the need for every member of the church, in whatever position, to be continually growing in his or her relationship with Jesus.

Growing in Depth

The limitations of the church building meant that, from the beginning, homes were used for various meetings, with all the advantages of a relaxed and informal atmosphere. From the start, the central, regular meeting of the church, besides that on a Sunday, was an evening fellowship for Bible study, prayer and praise. The lady who once publicly thanked the minister for his Bible study and then declared she had not understood a word of it did an invaluable service in emphasising the need to begin where people are and stay on the right level!

An ordinary living room was obviously limiting the size of the group, and enthusiastic singing late at night was not a very helpful witness to the neighbours, but the change from one central meeting to a pattern including more housegroups did not develop easily. We wanted, but did not know how to develop, small groups; in the end they developed almost by accident as we tried to meet the steady influx of people who had come to us lacking in basic teaching. We asked as many people as possible to commit themselves to four meetings entitled 'How to know God', 'How to pray', 'How to read the Bible' and 'How to witness'. These 'How' groups proved so helpful that people wanted to continue meeting in housegroups; these then were the start of our 'building blocks' for church growth.

A previously established 'link' group had a good record for adding new couples, enabling them to discuss their faith and encouraging them to pray together, and other groups quickly became training grounds for Christians following a set course of instruction, often linked with the Sunday teaching. Housegroup leaders were commissioned to encourage their group to come together, to support one another by practical and pastoral care and to be effective witnesses for Christ in the whole of their living.

As leadership began to be shared more widely, the question of authority opened up. It was important to seek out leadership, preaching and teaching gifts. This question came to a head in 1980 when the Bishop of Blackburn came to conduct a special commissioning service for housegroup leaders and for four of us as elders (he didn't like the term 'elders' and encouraged us to use the word 'leaders'.) The elders were commissioned to minister to the glory of Christ, specifically to lead the housegroups in their different geographical areas by providing pastoral care, and by teaching and building up the groups through the growing ministry of every member.

Among the leaders who met on Saturday mornings to pray and discuss the work was our first 'imported' leader; he was not home-grown or on the salaried staff. Terry Grew moved up from the South of England, and, deciding he wanted to make his spiritual home with us, looked for a house near the church—not an easy task in this particular area. For many months he was in Blackburn during the week and travelled back to London at weekends. During this time, he made a significant contribution to our mid-week fellowship and his teaching and pastoral gifts were quickly recognised. His sensitive approach to ministry made it much easier later on for others to be accepted as leaders. It is interesting to note that in less than five years all four of the original leaders have been called away from the church—through death, moving job and training for missionary service. The diocesan scheme for lay readers and pastoral auxiliaries has helped to raise new ones.

We soon discovered that annual confirmation/baptism classes were not enough to cope with newcomers. We experimented with the 'Saints Alive' training course which included a challenge to commitment. As soon as we had enough for a new group, we would start again, and at the end of each course, try to integrate members into the existing housegroup structure.

Organised groups were not the only means of growth. Books played a vital part. Blackburn is not particularly well served with Christian bookshops and a big investment of stock for a church bookstall quickly yielded an annual turnover of more than £1,500. Book sales were always boosted when titles coincided with preaching series. The Spirit gave to most parishioners—whether they were avid readers or not—the desire and thirst, to know more.

An important cassette ministry developed as the Sunday School teachers were supplied with the rest of the service on tape. They did not just want the ministry of the word, but every part of the worship, knowing how clearly God can speak through his people at worship. The demand for tapes of both morning and evening services was an unexpected sign that people were enjoying worship and keen not to miss anything. The man who started this ministry was someone who, when he heard the Good News, was angry that no-one had told him sooner. He then set out to make sure the same accusation was not levelled against him.

Equally important for growth were the various practical projects which naturally arose. The first was the decision to replace the fixed pews with new chairs—a large financial project which deepened the commitment of individuals, involving them personally, and which increased their faith in God as the job was completed. A car park, an extension to it, giving for the mission programme, maintaining the church grounds (and later, the vicarage garden!), helping with a monthly lunch for older folk and—to date—building and furnishing a new hall, have enabled people to learn about giving their time, money and talents, and in the process have brought a deepening bond of togetherness within the church family. Rotas developed in all directions for leading the prayers, choruses, crèche, helping in Sunday school. As numbers of children grew, more people came forward to teach and leaders for Pathfinders (the next step after Sunday school) emerged as the need arose. As people give in service, they invariably grow.

Growing Pains—the Cost of Spiritual Warfare

At first, the church was unbalanced by a large proportion of its members being immature Christians without any previous church background. As well as all the positive freshness and vitality of their contribution, their inexperience meant dramas were quickly made into crises and the same few people were called on repeatedly to help them through. Nor was hospitality something that came naturally, so we prayed for this gift to be given to the fellowship. Numbers for confirmation were not high and on one confirmation Sunday my small group was reduced still further at the eleventh hour, when just before 6.30 pm two lads came into the vestry and said that they were not ready! Fortunately, the Bishop was very understanding, and this kind of instability, as well as personal disappointment, has to be taken into account in a relatively new church.

The personal cost for Stanley Fell was life itself. Remembered for his zeal and love for his master, he had a concern so big that he denied himself days off and holidays to forward the work. He left in 1980 to take on a country parish. However, Stanley was never going to rust away, and having said farewell to his son and family as they set out for Zaire with the Leprosy Mission, he had a heart attack and died.

On a different level, we found it hard on family life to operate from a house on the estate. The one living room was frequently used for meetings, and there was little scope for private counselling. We often had to pray for protection for our children who had unavoidably witnessed distressing scenes. Fortunately the diocese had a cottage in nearby Kirkby Lonsdale and annual trips were like a touch of heaven. The Lord seemed to make each one better and renew us for the battle.

Not surprisingly, the battle was at its keenest around mission times. Before one mission we had the strangest combination of car accidents. At least six different cars within the fellowship were damaged, although nobody was hurt. Whenever we did any teaching about spiritual warfare we felt some comeback. On one occasion I was threatened physically on the estate, visited by the police and a reporter from the News of the World, and a letter full of extraordinary lies was sent to the Bishop. The hurtful part was that it felt as though the church authorities, too, were against us; and one of the suffragan bishops was sent round with Bible open to put me right. It took some time to win back his support, and only as he witnessed the gentle, united moving of the Spirit among the people were his fears allayed.

On the whole, the diocese was supportive, especially in terms of finance and administration. We were perhaps particularly vulnerable in that we did not have anyone dropping in to say 'How is it going? Can I pray with you about this vision' To be under pressure in a new situation can mean loneliness. Fortunately we had increasing fellowship within the church, but sometimes we would have appreciated encouragement from outside. Occasionally, we had to cope with the suspicion of sheep-stealing from other churches and until the new parish boundaries were properly sorted out, there were areas of tension. On reflection early 'understandings' between co-operating ministers should have been put on a more formal footing. Undoubtedly, when willing partners moved on, blockages arose.

Going on Growing

On April 1, 1982, Church of the Redeemer, Shadsworth, became the first new parish in the town for around 50 years. Its parish status was a recognition of its growth and gave the church a greater opportunity to serve the area. Once we had our own PCC we saw the limitations of trying to discuss everything in detail. An away-day at the Diocesan Retreat/Conference Centre led to the setting up of five working parties:

Mission—to oversee and stimulate involvement in missionary work (this was defined as Christian activity outside the parish, whether in the UK or overseas).

Building—to translate vision into reality and to communicate to the rest of the church ways of responding to the challenge of building a new church hall, and to care for all plant and land within the church premises.

Worship—to make sure that this important Christian activity is constantly renewed, ensuring we are glorifying the Lord and leading worshippers to an increased awareness of his presence with his people.

Mission England—to stimulate local church evangelism and all that was involved in preparation and training through Mission England.

Media—to oversee our communication (internal and external) through the written word as well as audio-visual resources; to review constantly our publicity and to encourage more effective communication of the gospel in this area of Blackburn.

It was hard work sorting out the terms of reference for

these working parties, but worth all the effort. By this stage, we were seeing a few more professional people emerge on the scene, but the qualification for the PCC was still spiritual awareness rather than academic or professional prowess.

On the ministry front we knew from Ephesians 4 that teaching and pastoral gifts were essential parts of our local ministry. Dorothy Beavan became our first pastoral auxiliary and set a good precedent tackling a growing need particularly in the pastoral care of the elderly. We tended to see the prophetic and evangelistic gifts as part of a more intinerant ministry and looked for visitors to help us in these ways.

We tried to tune into any wider strategy of evangelism and were whole-hearted about the Mission England project. Under the leadership of a deputy headmaster converted in the 1950s under Billy Graham, a mission committee did an effective piece of work in preparation and visitation, and in filling coaches for Anfield. Over 60 referrals came to us and nurture groups were positive. We were not so effective at integrating those people into the body of Christ, perhaps because we were not quick enough to discern a right avenue for service.

Our worship building has limited further growth, and it will be a big decision at some stage whether to knock down the back wall and extend, or set up a satellite church on the estate, which could possibly be an alternative church for young people freed from solvent abuse. A lot will depend on what housing if any, is built around the church. Meanwhile, the church has been stopped from growing fat by an accelerated exodus of people moving away to different parts of the country.

Week by Week

The piano and organ strike up together as folk pick their way between prams at the back. One church warden likened it to a local maternity hospital! For the first 15 minutes, the whole church family are in together with an emphasis on praise in worship. A chorus time may involve some of the children and often the person leading gives a word of testimony to God's present activity in their lives. The children then leave for Sunday school, Pathfinders or crèche in another building. Preserving the goodwill of the staff in the community centre has always been essential. This leaves a natural break in the service while we wait for parents to return from taking the under-three's to the crèche. This time may be used for sharing information about people or coming events, a book review, open prayer for the children with their teachers or any particular need. Occasionally, it seems right to have a long silent pause to be open to God and just to settle after the children have bounced out.

The basic pattern varies only slightly. Once a month we use 'Rite A' Holy Communion. There is also a monthly parade service when all but the crèche stay in for family worship. One book contains the format for both these services. We use *Hymns for Today's Church*, *Psalm Praise* and printed material on an overhead projector. The Anglican liturgy allows for much freedom, but within a sound framework.

The evening service has changed. In 1977, with an average of less than 15 people, the minister was home by 8 pm. Encouragement by Pat Westall to pray in faith for the Lord to increase the numbers, the introduction of coffee afterwards and a growing desire for worship without small distractions, has meant that numbers have swelled and the going-home time extended to 9, and then 10 pm. Another factor in the timing has been the bi-monthly service of prayer for healing with the laying on of hands. Set in the context of Holy Communion, the first opportunity saw 16 people come forward to receive this ministry.

At one stage, we felt that the morning parade service was getting too much for the older folk, so they were offered an earlier, quieter service of Holy Communion. Hardly anyone came. They voted with their feet and persisted in joining in with the rest of the family. They were thrilled to see younger people come in and want to stay. They were seeing the answer to their prayers.

From the first, the vision of Stanley Fell, allied with the preseverance to see it come about, helped by the costly sacrifice of the people of Christ Church, made for plans and structures that were ripe for development. For those at the heart of the new church, there were tears and laughter, trials as well as joys, but always the excitement that the living God was at work among us.

Chapter 3

Ichthus Christian Fellowship

1974

Roger Forster

Ichthus Christian Fellowship, located in south-east London, serves an inner city area comprised of local government housing estates, older private homes, and small industrial estates. From a congregation of 250 in 1980, Ichthus has expanded to a 1985 membership of over 1,000 people meeting in 15 different congregations.

The leading minister, Roger Forster, holds a degree in maths and theology and, before founding Ichthus, travelled in itinerant evangelism and Bible teaching. He used his home as a 'spiritual rescue shop'; it was out of these experiences, he says, that Ichthus Fellowship grew.

Roger and his wife Faith have three children. In his rare moments of leisure, he likes to walk and to read. As well as the author of this chapter, Roger is editor of this book.

Forest Hill lies in the twilight zone of London: that is, it is the run-down area you pass through on your way from the more affluent suburbs, like Bromley or Beckenham, to the concrete jungles of really depressed inner city areas like Brixton, Camberwell, Peckham and New Cross. It was in

Forest Hill that Ichthus Christian Fellowship began 11 years ago. My wife, Faith, and I had moved there five years earlier in response to a very clear leading from God. For me it was a return to my home town, for I grew up here. We had previously been involved in full-time evangelism and social action a little further out of London in Erith, Kent, where we had run our home as a rescue shop for all sorts of people in need, as well as engaging in more general Christian work.

When God led us to Forest Hill, we had no clear idea of what we were to do here. We joined a local church, and I pursued an itinerant ministry of evangelism and Bible teaching, whilst Faith concentrated on establishing a home for our children. A few years passed in this way, during which we settled and formed bonds of fellowship with a number of local Christians who prayed for us and our work.

During these years we saw many exciting things happen in a variety of areas of ministry, both in the United Kingdom and many other parts of the world. At times we formed teams of people, mainly students, to train and work with us in evangelising villages, towns and universities where I was invited to lead missions. I had a full and rewarding ministry but there was something unfulfilled within us. More and more we began to conceive and teach a vision for the people of God. We longed for the reality of a New Jerusalem-style society but had little opportunity to express it.

Our first clear guidance was to begin to form a team and after praying over several possibilities, Faith and I asked Roger and Sue Mitchell to leave their school teaching and join us full-time in evangelism. At the same time we got involved in the 1974 'Power Project', presented by the Evangelical Alliance. This was a programme of grassroots evangelism by local churches throughout the country. Roger Mitchell and I were invited to join the 'Power in Peckham' Committee as evangelists. Our aim was to stimulate and mobilise churches in South East London to go out to the masses of unreached people in the area with the message of the Lord Jesus.

We soon discovered other Christians in Forest Hill and Sydenham with a vision for evangelism, and by the time the project was over we found ourselves knit together with a small band of people who were keen to commit themselves to ongoing and concentrated evangelism in our area. Strange to say, we could not find a local church to share our enthusiasm, although we looked at and visited a number. For various reasons, evangelism was not high on the agenda for most churches at that time, despite the enormous need all around. Internal problems and discouragement had contributed to an inward-looking mentality in most churches; this inevitably militated against effective evangelism and growth.

Eventually our group asked me if I would lead them in evangelising our area in depth and in forming a new church to do it. Faith and I prayed it over for a month, and eventually committed ourselves in September 1974 to seeking God's kingdom in our immediate London housing areas. At that time we were a group of about 18 adults plus a few children. Our ages ranged from a new-born baby to two ladies aged 70 and 80 years respectively! These particular ladies have been a great source of blessing and strength to the work over the years. Though very frail now in body, they are still with us, rejoicing in what God has done.

Two middle-aged couples, the Mills and the Magers, both in their 50s at that time, were also a source of strength and stability in the Fellowship life, until the Lord led the Magers into Christian work abroad, and the Mills into retirement in Scotland. Both couples served as housegroup leaders and leaders of the Fellowship over many years and have a very special place in our hearts.

Before we formally began our work, I visited other local ministers to inform them of our intentions and received nothing but encouragement to go ahead. The housing areas we were going to concentrate on were not considered fruitful ground and local ministers had enough to do already; so their blessing was readily given. We have always worked hard to keep good relationships with other churches in any area we work in and usually support inter-church activities. Somehow my wife manages to run the local interdenominational branch of the Womens' World Day of Prayer as well, despite her already full schedule. Moreover, we have never encouraged people to leave their churches to come to us (though some have anyway), and we have given our blessing to those who have left to join other churches.

Two years ago, we also poured a great deal of time, manpower and money into the local expression of Mission to London, as south east London evangelical churches mounted a two-week mission in Blackheath with Eric Delve and Luis Palau. We were glad to use our evangelistic experience to lead others in this venture and have been concerned to demonstrate our commitment to the body of Christ regardless of denominational labels.

At our first formal meeting as a Fellowship, we set ourselves to choose a name. We finally came up with the name 'Ichthus', an ancient Greek acrostic for the titles of our Lord ('Jesus Christ, Son of God, Saviour'), which had the advantage of the visual symbol of the fish. At the time we saw it more as a name to 'tide us over' until we found premises which would lend their name to the group; however, that has never happened, and we have been Ichthus ever since. It is a tongue-twisting, typographically hazardous name, but it has survived nevertheless!

Early Days

Because we had a clear conviction that we were called to the work we were doing, we started off with the confidence that God was with us, and that we would see his kingdom extended in our area despite all odds. This deep assurance kept us going through the rough and seemingly barren patches at the beginning. Despite the first few months that brought waves of pressure and discouragement, we kept our little boat on course; and we found a lot of joy in seeing the possibility of dreams from the past at last realised.

From the beginning we had three aspects to our church life, born partly out of our biblical understanding and partly out of experience. The first aspect was, of course, our *fellowship* together. We determined to commit ourselves to one another and share our lives as fully as we could. Any success we may have had in our history has grown out of a fellowship of love and commitment to one another. To laugh and cry together, to be loyal in word and deed: these are still basic to our church life, though today this would be most fully expressed in our housegroups and congregations. (It is harder to create fellowship in large-scale gatherings, but we do work at it nonetheless by rotating leaders regularly round the congregations.) Weekends away, fun events, pastoral care, and sharing of lives all help to keep such fellowship alive.

The second aspect is *mission*. This is written into our Trust Deed as a major part of the purpose of the Fellowship. We take seriously the Great Commission and see mission, evangelism and social action not as 'para-church activities' to be left to special societies distinct from the church, but as an integral part of our church life. From the beginning we have engaged not only in continuous evangelism and social action in our area, but also in active participation in overseas mission. Besides sending many overseas missionaries, several of our leaders have themselves been involved in mission, serving the Lord for extended periods of time in countries such as India, Turkey, the South Pacific and Cyprus.

Others of us, at one time or another, have entered into areas of social action in this country, opening our homes to alcoholics, drug addicts, delinquents and disturbed people. This policy helped equip us to lead the social action programme called 'Jesus Action', which Ichthus operated almost from our beginning. It is fundamental to our strategy that all our leaders should have evangelistic gifts or vision, so that the church does not turn in on itself too much.

The third aspect of our church life is *training*. If we are to produce Christian workers, able to face the challenge and pressures of the secular and hostile environment in which we live, they will need to be trained 'on the job'—which seems to have been our Lord's method. We built this objective into our fundamental understanding of who we were. We wanted ordinary men and women to find themselves part of an army of workers who need not feel ashamed or put down when confronted by non-Christians, but who are equipping themselves to advance with the gospel.

From the beginning we began taking on 'trainees' in evangelism and church planting, at first one at a time, then in small groups, until now we have a carefully organised training programme called 'Network'. It still functions as an integral part of the local church, however, which means that the church is teaching the Networkers, even as the

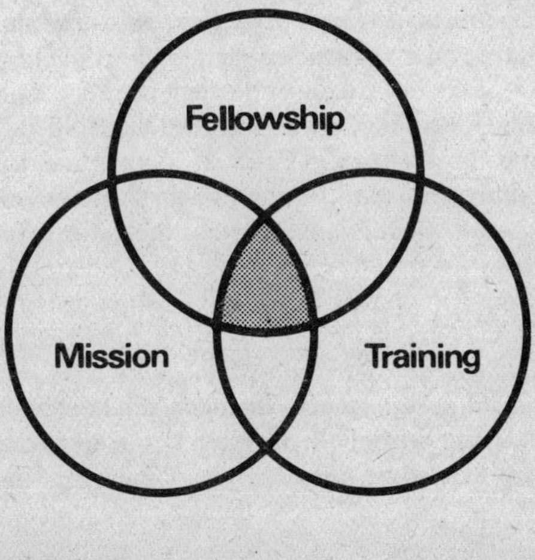

Networkers take a lead in the outreach of the church. We also take other groups of people for short-term training periods during the year.

These three aspects of church life are in dynamic tension all the time, keeping us alive and stimulated, and preventing us from stagnation. It can be seen in the diagram on p. 53. The shaded area represents the heart of the church where all three circles overlap and are supervised by the leadership.

Three Principles

Having talked about the basic aspects of our Church life, it is worth recording three principles or resolutions that we adopted at the very inception of Ichthus as we sought God's way forward as a small group together.

The first was *love*. Jesus said, 'All men will know that you are my disciples if you love one another' (John 13:35). (Could this be the reason Satan attacks love in the church? It is a powerful evangelistic aid.) Most of us had experienced previous church situations where rampant back-biting, mistrust and hostility had flourished even among the leaders. The resulting hurt and damage to the flock of God is incalculable. We recognised that human beings are prone to fall out of love with one another so we simply made a commitment to love one another and to build relationships of trust and forgiveness. We talked about this quite openly, and held one another to it when testing times came. Several years ago Faith wrote a poem for our leaders, two lines of which read:

Let forgiveness be unfailing,
be that loving presence still.

The second was *humility*. Perhaps I have given the impression that we knew all the answers from the beginning, but we did not—and we do not. Whilst we have had a fairly clear strategy in our church planting no one should take that to mean that we have a pat answer to every problem and situation. The sheer complexity of life and humanity means that we are constantly faced with problems to which only the fresh wisdom of the Holy Spirit can give us the answer. We are not ashamed to say 'I don't know, but I will pray about it.'

The third was *openness to the Holy Spirit.* We all agreed at the beginning that we were still learners in the spiritual life, and that we very much wanted more of the Lord and of his Holy Spirit. We determined not to get bogged down by dead traditions or sterile rituals, but to keep our church structures, as well as ourselves, flexible and able to be changed and remoulded by the Holy Spirit.

We still keep one another to that resolve, even though we sometimes joke that the only way the leadership keeps up with the changes is by attending the regular newcomers evenings when our structures are explained to the uninitiated! My wife also hints darkly that we will soon need to issue a personal computer with each guest card handed out, so that 'newies' can keep track of our activities! However, life is characterised by change; we want to be alive in the Holy Spirit as individuals and as a church.

First Meeting Place

These principles were all hammered out together in the first weeks of our fellowship's life in the autumn of 1974, while we were meeting in the front room of my house on Wednesdays and Sundays. Soon we decided to 'go public' and hired the only building we could find at that time: a small clubroom, seating 50 people, right on the housing estate which we counted as our first target area, 200 yards from my home.

As the hall was rather tatty looking, we began by gaining permission to redecorate it; our first real fellowship times in our new premises were over the paintbrushes and rollers and endless cups of tea! It was not an ideal place to start a church—our careful paintwork was soon marred by the karate club and beery parties held there at other times—but we found happiness together turning it into our first Fellowship home. We celebrated our first Christmas with a carol service for which we visited every home on the estate and neighbourhood with invitations, and with a Fellowship party in my home with lots of laughter, food and fun. Both occasions were successful in their aims.

We began gaining new members almost immediately, with one or two converts and a few Christians who felt led to join us as they saw what we were doing. Some of the latter did not stay, as the hard foundational work that we were engaged in was less appealing than a comfortable established church, but those who did join us and stick with us because they shared our vision and ideals are still with us today. One of the blessings that Faith and I constantly marvel at, and give thanks for, is the quality of the people whom God has joined to us; our co-workers have become our closest friends. Besides Roger and Sue Mitchell, Arthur and Ella Mills and Jim and Polly Mager, there were John and Yvonne Pressdee and Phil and Merrie Reynolds, who were also all founder members. John is on our central leadership today, having left his secular work to give himself full-time to our evangelism and nurture group work, while Phil leads one of our congregations. Alistair Crow, a solicitor, and his wife Lily, joined us about a year after our inception. Al is still one of our leaders today.

Leadership

At the beginning, we formed an *ad hoc* committee to handle the Fellowship affairs until leaders clearly emerged. After two years, I visited every member of the Fellowship (60–70 people) to discover whom they recognised as their leaders.

Eventually we publicly recognised the men whom the Fellowship had chosen. There was unanimity in the choice. This group began meeting every Monday from 8 pm until about 11.30 pm, praying together and seeking the Lord's way ahead as a leadership.

At that time, four of the group were in secular employment and two (myself and Roger Mitchell) were in full-time Christian work. In 1977, Ray Mayhew, another full-time worker with exceptional pastoral gifts, joined the Fellowship and married Jenny who was working with us part-time as a pastoral worker. In 1978, Ray was included in the leadership while Jenny 'retired' for a while to raise a family!

As the years have rolled on the work has grown so rapidly that we have changed the patterns of our leadership meetings, and also the structure of leadership. We now have a leadership of six full-time workers (including Faith, who was eventually recognised as a leader) and Graham Warner, who joined us in 1976. Only one leader is in secular employment today and his role in the church is more pastoral now. The executive decisions are largely made by the full-time leadership group—necessary because of the size and complexity of the work. We meet all day on Mondays to deal with Fellowship business and to assess needs.

In addition to the basic leadership (elders) we have a ministry team (prophets) which includes most of the leadership but adds several others. Sue Mitchell is one. She heads our flourishing overseas mission department. Ken McGreavy is another. He came to join us a few years ago and has been particularly developing a healing ministry. Graham Kendrick, who has an exceptional prophetic ministry in song, joined us a year ago. More recently, Kofi Osafo, a Ghanaian by birth, but with experience in inner-city work in London, was added to us. All members of the ministry team regularly preach in our congregations. They also all look to the Lord to supply their needs to some extent, since the Fellowship cannot fully support so many. Instead, the church makes over a lump sum for ministry each month; it is divided among the leadership and ministry team according to need.

Ichthus Christian Workers

Besides the leadership and ministry team, we have 16 full-time evangelists and church planters called Ichthus Christian Workers. They live by faith in a similar way to the ministry team. They are all graduates of our Network training programme, and they pioneer our new works and congregations with the help of current Networkers. All Networkers and ICWs are assigned to area teams under a member of the ministry team.

Administration

At the beginning the leaders handled all administrative matters themselves, including finances, with the able help of a general secretary, Lynne Sainty. This arrangement continued for years, with different leaders having different areas of administration such as: pastoral, financial, evangelistic, training and stewarding. But three years ago we recognised that we desperately needed a full-time administrator. After several months of prayer, we invited Mike Oakes, a senior social worker, to leave his secular employment and join us.

Mike did so and has proved his worth, not just in immediately taking over the administrative needs on all fronts, but in training others. Today he heads a small but highly efficient administrative team made up of workers who handle all aspects of administration. Mike meets with the leadership every Monday to see that all decisions made are activated. He also supervises the running of the Ichthus office, which is the hub of Fellowship life and activity.

Ichthus House

For the first few years, Ichthus depended on rented buildings and leaders' homes as the focal points of the Fellowship. However, as the work grew, it became obvious that we needed some sort of base which would be accessible all the time. Together we began to pray and give and—with the help of Christians outside the Fellowship—we were able to secure a large Edwardian house near my home for use as the Fellowship house, office and training centre. Today it is primarily used for the latter two purposes, with an additional administrative office in a member's neighbouring home. Currently we have 29 Networkers training with us for a year in evangelism and church-planting.

As far as Sunday meeting places were concerned, when we had outgrown our original tiny rented hall after a few months, we moved our meetings firstly to a small Quaker Meeting place nearby, seating up to 100 people, and then, as we continued to grow, into a German Lutheran Church building, which we had felt from the beginning was ideal for our needs. It was right in the centre of our patch, seats 320 people, and is a bright modern building, if a little formal in design and layout. The Lutheran Church Council agreed to us using their premises since they only used it themselves twice a month. One of those occasions, one Sunday morning a month, acted as a spur to implement our housegroup system, and we began meeting in housegroups for fellowship and food on that Sunday each month.

The Structure of the Fellowship

In Ichthus today we have fellowship on a three-tier level. First, there is the cell or housegroup, where intimate fellowship and pastoral care take place. One Sunday morning a month and two Wednesday evenings, we meet in housegroups for prayer and Bible study, and usually a communal meal. Housegroups are made up of 12 to 20 people, plus children, and are loosely geographical in composition. The housegroup leader might be a single man or woman or a married couple in equal partnership, or sometimes a married person leading with their partner assisting. This is decided on the evidence of pastoral gifts and according to the time a person can commit.

Every housegroup leader has one or two assistants in any case, some of whom are in the process of being trained to start a new housegroup. We now have about 56 housegroups. Although the housegroups are primarily pastoral in function, they are expected to keep up an evangelistic vision also, and some are effective evangelistic units in their own right. Ray Mayhew, who heads up pastoral care in the Fellowship, recently summarised a list of housegroup leaders' responsibilities, which it might be useful to include here.

Housegroup leader's or leaders' responsibilities

Pastoral responsibilities

—have personal contact with each person in your group at least every month (visit, telephone, invite for meal)
—ensure that everyone in the group is remembered in prayer as effectively as possible
—assess needs of the children in your group and seek to meet them
—be aware of those with special needs (unemployed, single parents, handicapped)
—inform the pastoral team of people who need special visits (eg those in hospital)
—if people have particular counselling needs, contact the pastoral team for a 'surgery'
—recommend people to the leadership for baptism (check

with their Start Rite leader or congregational leader; go through the 'Believe and Be Baptised' booklet)
—teach tithing and financial stewardship (and practise it yourself!)

Evangelistic responsibilities

—encourage and train people in personal evangelism
—plan creative, evangelistic activities as a group (home meetings, street parties etc.)
—regularly participate as a group in the open air meetings of your congregation
—encourage active involvement in all the congregation and Ichthus-wide evangelistic events (missions etc.)
—set goals in 'conversion growth' (as distinct from 'transfer growth') for the group

Training and development responsibilities

—train people in the exercise and development of spiritual gifts
—integrate people into effective and fulfilling areas of service in the Fellowship
—train and develop others in housegroup leadership (do not appoint an assistant leader without prior consultation with the leadership)
—attend our six-monthly leadership weekends and other training events organised
—read as much as you can in the area of small group leadership (book list available)

Administrative responsibilities

—prayerfully and creatively plan the Sunday and Wednesday housegroup meetings (transport, welcoming, music, leading, catering, etc.)
—plan creative social activities for the group

—every three months give an updated list of your housegroup members to the pastoral team and your congregational leader
—meet regularly with your assistant leaders for prayer and planning
—keep informed of special events in the Fellowship and bring them to the attention of your group (appoint a housegroup administrator if necessary)
—appoint a 'whip', to telephone new and fringe people to remind them of when and where the group meets
—appoint a Jesus Action rep for the group
—appoint a missionary rep for the group

General responsibilities

—familiarise yourself with the history and distinctives of Ichthus (tapes are available)
—attend the monthly meetings with the leadership (the Monday immediately before the fourth Sunday)
—meet with a member of the pastoral team to discuss the progress/problems of your group (once a month)
—serve as a counsellor on the Tuesday 'surgeries' as required
—assist in praying for people on Sunday nights at Sedgehill School
—make sure visitors to your congregation/Sedgehill are welcome and linked into a housegroup

NB: There is a tape available of the training session which develops in detail each area of responsibility.

As you can see, our housegroup leaders need to be energetic people, and they are. They are a fundamental part of our leadership structures and we concentrate a lot of prayer and thought on them. As ministry team members, we are all overloaded with demands on our time, but we try to give immediate priority to any housegroup leader who needs to see us for whatever reason. We also hold regular training days for them and keep in touch as closely as possible with their needs.

The second tier of fellowship life is the *congregation*, which in our case has grown from the original single congregation into a network of 15 different congregations ranging in size from 30 to 200 people, the fruits of our church-planting in various inner city areas. We began church-planting from our central resource congregation three years ago using the ministry team, Networkers and Ichthus Christian workers to pioneer our new work. We do not normally start a congregation until at least two housegroups are already meeting and functioning effectively in the area, as these form the basis of the new congregational life.

The congregations meet three Sunday mornings, one Sunday evening and one Wednesday evening per month. The Sunday morning meeting is the family service, informal, aimed at all ages, with simple basic teaching and plenty of visual aids. Children are especially catered for and the service is suitable to bring non-Christians or new Christians too. Most congregations serve coffee after the service and this gives an opportunity to chat with newcomers, pick up on pastoral needs, and sometimes to pray with individuals.

The two evening meetings of the congregations have a slightly different slant. At these, the congregations worship in a deeper way and the gifts of the Spirit, prophecy, healing, deliverance and suchlike, are more likely to be in evidence.

The area church consisting of a number of congregations is not new. The Methodist movement, among many others, practised it, and some of us see the church at Ephesus as the hub from which other congregations are spawned off into Colossae, Hierapolis, Laodicea, as well as possibly the remaining churches of the Book of Revelation.

The third tier of Fellowship life is *celebration*. Three Sunday evenings a month, the congregations all gather together in a local comprehensive school for worship, communion and prophetic ministry. On the fourth week of the month, we meet on the Saturday evening instead of Sunday for our celebration and extend an invitation to other local churches to join us for worship and teaching. We often have a visiting speaker on these latter occasions.

The advantage of large-scale celebration gatherings is the inspiration they minister to Christians—to know and feel that they are part of something bigger than just the 60 or 70 people at congregational meetings. The supernatural is often released in the large-scale gatherings, and people experience something more of the power and presence of God.

Evangelism and Teaching

Our converts are won in various ways. Some might be first befriended by another Christian and introduced into the friendship network of their housegroup. Others might be contacted from evangelistic outreaches (door-to-door or in the open air) and invited to a congregational family service. Some are introduced to the church by means of our special guest services at Christmas or Easter or through a friendship evening, such as a barn dance or a 'gospel night out'. When people show some interest in the faith but seem to need more time to consider it, they might be invited to join an 'enquirers' class' at which Christianity is explained informally with no pressure applied to respond.

However, if they have actually made a step of commitment they would be invited to join a Start Rite class in order to begin immediate instruction in the faith. These are usually held in someone's home and consist of informal groups of six to ten people who are all new Christians learning together. Many of these groups are so successful that members are reluctant to stop meeting after the course is completed (usually in three months)!

In addition to Start Rite, as a new believer gets more sure of his or her faith, he or she is usually linked with a more mature Christian, one-to-one. Together they study the person of Jesus through Mark's Gospel so that the new convert becomes fully a disciple of Jesus Christ himself. Using some notes my wife has prepared on Mark's Gospel, the mature person aims to teach the converts how to learn from Jesus through his word and how to apply the word to their lives in everyday practical living. Often the particular problems and needs of the new Christian are aired and shared most fully in this sort of relationship. By the end of a year we hope the convert will be fully integrated into church life.

In our early days, when converts came in ones and twos rather than a number at one time, their first follow-up was through one-to-ones. However, now we find it more effective to make Start Rite groups the first step, and a one-to-one the second. For more mature Christians who want to study more deeply the word of God in small groups, we also have FISH (Forward Into Spiritual Health) groups available.

Signs and Wonders

We are concerned to provide a solid base to our life together by means of regular, careful teaching of the Word of God. However, we want the supernatural aspects of our faith to be experienced too. 'Signs and wonders' might sound a pretentious designation for the healings, deliverance and supernatural manifestations of God's presence among us, but we certainly aim at the supernatural being natural and, of course, super in our life together!

George, now in his 80s, was an ex-policeman, commando and atheist, confined by illness to a wheelchair. One of our workers visited him regularly. George welcomed the chat and one day said to him, 'I guess I had better ask this Jesus into my life.' 'I guess you had better,' our man replied. George prayed, and as he did so got out of his wheelchair, then exclaimed, 'Goodness me, what have I done?' He later told us that he had seen a vision of Jesus and had stood up into Jesus' arms and was healed.

In another area, one of our workers said 'Lord, we have a special outreach time on Sunday morning, but I have visited these tower blocks and houses so many times. Where do you want me to go today?' He received the word 'No. 8'. It was where Esme lived. Yes, she wanted to come to the meeting. It was years since she had been to church. Our worker collected her next Sunday. As I preached in that congregation during the morning, Esme wept.

I sat down next to her afterwards. 'Would Jesus come into my life?' she asked. I replied 'Yes of course.' She added 'Would he take this pain from the surgical pin in my arm?' 'I am sure he wants to,' I said. 'Come, let's ask him.' We prayed. Jesus came in and the pain had gone by the afternoon. Esme came to every meeting after that and on the first few occasions loved to hold up her hand above her shoulder, which she had been unable to do before. This was also to say that she would like to give her testimony as to what Jesus had done for her. Her next visit to the hospital resulted in the doctors' leaving things untouched because she could now use her arm perfectly. On the second visit she was discharged without further treatment. They had X-rayed her arm and then remarked, 'We cannot find the pin.'

A Muslim family moved into a street where two members of the Fellowship befriended them. One day their baby was ill, and they turned to the Christian couple for help. They prayed for the child and he was promptly healed. The father and mother are now baptised and other members of the family are interested in the gospel.

These tangible manifestations of God's presence occur not only at our central celebration times but may be seen from the examples given in the overall life of the church. However we are concerned that from week to week that sense of his presence in our meetings does not decrease. If this appears to be the case we give ourselves to prayer that we might go 'ever further and deeper into the heart of God'. We have not always had so many manifestations as we see today, although we have always prayed for the sick, and significant breakthroughs have occurred at various points in our history, lifting the church to a higher level of expectancy. These fresh levels of expectancy the new converts seem to walk into and accept easily, whereas others of us have struggled to rise to them.

One of our founder members had a tumour on the brain diagnosed a number of years ago. We anointed him with oil and prayed together for him as a Fellowship. I hesitatingly prophesied over him and added the words 'Wouldn't it be good if. . .?' When he returned to the hospital for an investigatory operation a few days later they could find no evidence of the growth, and later in writing to him used almost the same words that I had used in praying but without the cautious preface.

A few years later, my own son was miraculously healed from cancer through prayer and the laying on of hands. In many ways the whole episode marked a spiritual breakthrough for us all. It came upon us very suddenly during a time of intense spiritual pressure. We had made fresh breakthroughs in evangelism and the enemy plainly did not like it. At this time, a threat and a curse addressed to me personally was painted anonymously on our church wall in large letters and signed 'Son of Satan'. Whatever the link may be we will probably never know for sure, but shortly afterwards my son, then fifteen years old, began to experience breathlessness and pain in the chest.

This was wrongly diagnosed at first as a chest infection. Another month elapsed with Chris getting worse before my wife finally got him a chest X-ray and this showed massive enlargement of lymph glands in the chest; he was rushed to Guy's Hospital and within a few days we received the grim news. He was diagnosed as suffering from a rapidly growing leukaemic-type cancer which had already spread throughout the lymphatic system and had entered the spinal fluid. His prognosis in medical eyes was very poor. Despite the indescribable shock and pain we experienced at this news, the Lord gave us clarity and strength to walk through this valley of shadows with him. It came at a time when many of the leaders were away. However, Ray Mayhew responded immediately and sensitively to the crisis and began mobilising prayer wherever he possibly could, both within the Fellowship and further afield. Then together we called for a day of prayer and fasting for the whole Fellowship a few days later—less than a week from the discovery of the disease.

Meanwhile we were put in touch with a brother from the United States, who was visiting this country, and who had seen miracles of healing in his own ministry. He agreed to come with us into the hospital to pray for our son on the day of fasting and prayer. Other groups, particularly the participants at Spring Harvest, were also standing with us in prayer especially on that day. Together we touched the heavens on Chris's behalf and saw a dramatic breakthrough. By the next day all his symptoms had vanished, and from that day to this no cancer cell has been found in his body.

Nonetheless the hospital was reluctant to agree that a healing had taken place and it was a long while before they acknowledged that no malignant cells could be found. Meanwhile they insisted that he receive chemotherapy as planned so it was months before the trauma of treatment was over for Chris. But the most important thing was that he was healed and today, nearly four years later, he knows that God has powerfully touched his life. The church also grew spiritually, as did Faith and I, as we all discovered the power of prayer, the meaning of love and commitment and the importance of unity.

Our growth in God as a Fellowship has not been without such traumas and evidences of satanic opposition, but we are learning to use the power and name of Jesus to destroy all the works of the evil one. As we reinvade the inner city we are more and more aware of the need to deal with the demonic and to secure protection from Christ.

Jesus Action

Jesus did supernatural things, like feeding the 5,000 and raising the dead, but he also spent time with the children and washed feet. Jesus Action is the name of the social action arm by which we serve into the community. Just as Jesus said that the works he did his Father was doing through him, so we believe Christ's hand is in us, doing good works and bringing glory to the Father (Matthew 5:16). These works are very different from humanistic activities and aims. We want to reveal and leave Jesus behind when we have finished serving.

An elderly woman's home was flooded out on one occasion. Our workers cleaned up and dried out her property. Her grand-daughter, in her 30s, knocked on my door later with the words, 'are you the folk who helped my grandmother? I want to know more about this kind of Christianity.' Some times we have put on meals and entertainment in drama and song for the elderly, and on these occasions we also share our faith in the Lord. Many of these people will not venture out at night for the fear of being mugged and will only come if we collect them for such an occasion. When I took one lady back to her flat, she said to me, 'If God is like that I want more of him.'

Sometimes people make a direct appeal to us to help them by means of Jesus Action. At other times they are referred to us by members of the Fellowship, by the Social Services, or by similar bodies. Currently we have more general areas of social action operating, such as housing co-operatives and an unemployment project.

'Into All the World'

Perhaps I should add that our outward looking in evangelism is not just confined to the shores of the United Kingdom. We have always kept world mission before us and have encouraged our people to consider the Third World and to be prepared for overseas service of various kinds. For several years now we have had more than 40 people serving abroad in evangelism with various agencies, in relief work, medical work and church-planting. Sue Mitchell ably handles the administration and inspiration for this side of the work; she has initiated prayer cells for different areas of the world, mission focus days and with her colleagues on the missions committee, has come up with a strategy for extending our church-planting activities to areas abroad. Though we have a large missionary budget, it is inevitably far too small to meet all the needs!

As we look back over the past 11 years of church-planting we see a complicated tapestry of human and divine life and activity woven together in our Fellowship and family life. We have all gained from the experience and have grown in our ministries as we have talked and prayed together, learned from one another and drawn more deeply on the resources of Christ. Our own children, too, have been blessed and enriched by the experience of Fellowship life and growth, even though at times they have felt resentful at the intrusions into our family life and privacy and the demands on our time. Our two older children, now aged 19 and 17 respectively, can barely remember any other church life than Ichthus. As for Debbie (8) she was born into the business, so to speak! They have always felt part of the work.

Our son, Chris, was 10 years old when we prayed for finances to purchase the church house. He promptly emptied his money box into the fund so that, in his own words, 'I can feel that a little part of the house is there because of me.' Indeed, all the members of Ichthus who have prayed and loved and shared their lives can say the same. A little part of God's spiritual house is there because of them. It is this same encouragement that lifts our hearts as we look back at what God has done and look forward to far greater things yet. There is still much ground to be possessed, so we press forward with our learner plates still in place, but with confidence in our hearts that he is 'able to do immeasurably more than all we ask or imagine, according to his power that is at work within us, to him be glory . . .'! (Ephesians 3:20).

Chapter 4

Anfield Road Fellowship

1983

Dave Cave

Anfield Road Fellowship was formed in 1983 and from 10 members in that year has grown to over 40 in two years. Although associated with the United Reformed Church, Anfield is independent.

Under the Reverend Dave Cave the fellowship seeks to reach out to its inner city surroundings: to serve the local unemployed and especially youngsters on drugs.

Dave was brought up in Wales and educated at Congregational College and Manchester University. Though he is full-time minister of Anfield Road Fellowship, Dave is actually unpaid, the work being supported by his wife Tina, who is a haematologist. He and Tina have two sons, and Dave is the author of the recently published book Jesus Is Your Best Mate. *Among his hobbies he lists music, reading and—like several other ministers in this book—tropical fish.*

Life on the dole is hard to bear
But why should I begin to care?
When things get bad and really tough
That's when I reach for that fatal stuff.
I climb into my own magic bubble,

Just sit and stare, not aware of any trouble.
People warned me every day
I told them, there's no other way.
For my habit I rob and lie,
Bring heartache home, but I get by;
'Cause I know when I'm full of smack
There's no way I can turn back.
I cannot eat, I cannot sleep, I scream in pain
I've got this craving, my life will never be
the same again.
All I want is just the smack,
I wish I could turn the clock back.
I feel it running through my veins,
It's got the power to take away the pains.
Here I am in my own magic bubble,
All smacked up, I've got no trouble.
My life is ending, there is no doubt;
'Help me, please,' I've got to shout.
So let my corpse my message be,
If you're a smackhead, you'll end up like me.

(Written by a local 19-year-old heroin addict, who has since come off heroin and become a member of the fellowship)

Heroin is just one of the problems of Anfield, with unemployment running at eight people out of ten, a crime rate (80% drug-related) increasing all the time, and a level of diet which now reveals that the average height of young people in our area is less than the rest of Liverpool. All are symptoms of a depressed community which desperately needs good news.

The traditional Christian picture of the city is one of a place of evil with which God wants nothing to do and which godly people should avoid. At least, that is the first impression—but not what the Bible has to say. Abraham was originally a city-dweller in Ur (Genesis 11:31) and although he spent most of his life wandering through the land of

Canaan, Abraham had his heart set on another city: 'He was looking to the city with foundations, whose architect and builder is God' (Hebrews 11:10). Jesus wept over the city of Jerusalem, 'If you, even you, had only known on this day what would bring you peace—but now it is hidden from your eyes' (Luke 19:41–42). When Philip went to the principal city of Samaria and shared the good news, 'With shrieks, evil spirits came out of many, and many paralytics and cripples were healed. So there was great joy in that city' (Acts 8:7).

Then again the apostle Paul spent most of his time in the big cities of the Roman Empire—Ephesus, Philippi, Corinth, Thessalonica, Antioch, Athens, and Rome itself. Scripture strongly suggests that God loves the cities. He was prepared to save Sodom for the sake of just ten righteous, godly people (Genesis 18:32). So it can be seen why here in Anfield we believe that Liverpool is one of the cities God loves, and that if the cities can be reached so can the rest of this nation—but, as in the book of Acts, our first priority for mission must be the cities.

Anfield Road Fellowship began with a vision for the city. I have spent the whole of my ministry working in the city, listening to Christians apologising for the closure of churches, making excuses for the decline of mission to the inner city, and yet at the same time feeling that God has something powerful and positive to proclaim to the urban scene. The only way to encourage people to see what God can do, it seems to me, is to get on with it, and work out the vision. As I said in my book *Jesus is your Best Mate* (Marshalls, 1985):

> Institution must be the servant of Divine inspiration. Without the reality and presence of Jesus in the power of His Holy Spirit, worship, community, and denominations become just like Ezekiel's vision, a valley full of dry bones (Ezekiel 37:1–14), and the worst qualities of institution with-

> out inspiration emerge; inertia, self-satisfaction, worship of buildings, inward-looking, and a lack of love.

The vision for us came through Graham Cook, a URC minister, speaking at a meeting in Liverpool on Jesus' need for a donkey to take him into the city and the challenge that Jesus still needs donkeys to take him back into the cities of our land today.

The vision began to come into focus when a house in Anfield Road came on to the open market. We as a family were already prepared to respond to God's call to establish a new Church in the inner city, and the house seemed made-to-measure for our needs. We (and the building society) went ahead and purchased 86 Anfield Road.

The house is just up the road from Liverpool football ground in an area of cobble-stoned streets and terraced houses, most of which were well over 50 years old (No. 86 was built in 1885). The area was originally a very strong Protestant community, and although this is not as noticeable now as it used to be, many of the established families of the area still hold a strong affiliation to the Orange Lodge.

Small Beginnings

The work began in November 1983, when we held our first Christian meeting at No. 86, along with seven other people, all local 'Scousers'. Andy and Debbie, and Sue and Dave were two teenage couples—Andy and Debbie are now married. Then there was a married couple, Denny and Barbara; and Beryl, married, but coming along on her own. Beryl had spent a number of years in the Mormon church before coming to know Christ personally.

We set ourselves a number of tasks. We as a fellowship would avoid owning any buildings. We had seen too many inner-city churches struggling with that particular mill-stone.

We would not seek to pay for ministry. Firstly, because we could not afford to; and secondly, because of the danger of maintaining a one-man band approach to ministry. Partly connected with this was my own decision not to seek employment but not to sign on the 'dole' either, because I was and still am full-time for God. Financially, Tina, my wife, earned sufficient just to cover our living costs.

Although Anfield Road Fellowship was not denominational, some of us had belonged to the URC for some years previously and felt it right to try to establish denominational links, starting with the URC.

We would avoid as far as possible what we viewed as a middle-class structure of committees and meetings in order to allow most decision-making to be done in a more informal family model, always making sure that the Holy Spirit had number one priority in what was decided.

A main part of our mission on the Anfield Road would be not to compete with existing churches but rather to complement them. It was vital to us that we began a 'Heineken' ministry reaching out to those folk whom other Christians do not reach.

On the grounds that 'small is beautiful' and you can only effectively relate to about as many people who can fill a large front room, we felt that if Anfield Road Fellowship grew too big we would split on the amoeba principle, in order to allow for further growth and meaningful fellowship and support.

That is how we began, and it did not take very long for things to start happening. The Friday after our first meeting I received a late night 'phone call from Lin, from a local Baptist Church. She had a young man at her home who needed help and Lin felt Anfield Road Fellowship might have the answer. She brought him round at midnight and we talked. It turned out Graham was a 17-year old drug addict and pusher. He had been in constant trouble with the police, never managed to stay anywhere for very long, and was constantly on the move. But God had begun to challenge his life through the influence of Christians. Graham did not know how to handle this, and the Christians he knew did not know how to handle him.

We talked and prayed, and off they went. At 2.30 am the following morning, he was back, knocking on our door. He had taken a large dose of drugs and was having a weird 'trip'. Graham was convinced that it was the night of Jesus' return and he had got to get right with God, and that Dave Cave was the guy to talk to. It is not easy to counsel with any degree of clarity at that time of the morning and it was not made any easier by Graham's insistence on sleeping on our doorstep! I sat up and eventually he went home but was back bright and early for our Sunday morning meeting. During the meeting some of us laid hands on Graham (best known in our area as 'Buster') and our first new convert joined Anfield Road in the second week of its existence.

Two years later, Graham is still very much with us and has developed an amazing ministry as a local evangelist with a gift of discernment that brings him into all sorts of situations. Like the time he was arrested by the police for speaking to a local street gang about Jesus and booked for obstruction. We sent him to see a Christian solicitors' firm down the road. (We have an arrangement whereby we send them anyone with a legal problem and they send us anyone with a spiritual one, it works well.) While Graham was talking to John, he ended up chatting to John's secretary, and discovered she was not a Christian. With no more ado, he invited her to No. 86. That Sunday she came and brought her friend Julie. The meeting that day ended with Graham and Sue from our fellowship praying for both of them, and they were added to our group. A few weeks later John's secretary (also called Sue) brought along her cousin Tony, a boxer, and within the space of a week he was demanding to become a Christian.

Growth

Since then a number of people have tasted of the kingdom of God through the work of Anfield Road. John, who is in his mid-30s, was a cough medicine addict. Brian, who had spent the last 25 years in heavy drinking, and found his way to us from a men's hostel in Anfield Road. Dave, 'Tinhead', had been a local gang leader. Not everyone makes it, and sometimes folk come along for a month or two and then drift off—but even those who drift are rarely completely out of touch and we try to make the effort to maintain contact without any judgmental overtones, but just simply to let them know that their 'giving it a rest' does not mean that we do not care.

A pattern is beginning to emerge which suggests that some folk need what we call a 'wilderness experience'. After all, Moses went out into the wilderness before he was ready to go back to Egypt in response to God's call (Exodus 2:15–16). Elijah ran off into the desert to 'get away from it all' (I Kings 19:4). Jesus himself found it necessary to go out into the wilderness and face temptation before he could begin his public ministry (Matthew 4:1), and the apostle Paul went to Arabia for a time before he began his missionary journeys (Galatians 1:17).

Our experience with a few folk now has been that they have made an initial response to the good news of Jesus, after a month or two have drifted, but then come back (some within a few months, others after a year), even stronger than before. This was true of Steve, for instance, who turned up a few times but then disappeared altogether—now he has become very much a part of God's family at Anfield Road and is engaged to Sue.

Sue herself is a great encouragement to us. She is a local girl who has felt that God has called her to be a social worker living in the area where she works, which is Anfield. At present she is in her final year of training at polytechnic. The significance of this is that so often professional workers in our area—youth workers, probation officers, social workers, doctors and so on—live outside the area which they serve and often move on after only two or three years 'on the patch'. But we believe God is calling Christian professional workers to live where they work, in order to build up a stronger relationship with the local population, and that the Christian community must be a community within the community in order to give those workers the support they need as well as to be witnesses of the good news of Jesus Christ.

The life of the fellowship has developed in a number of ways over the past couple of years. We meet at No. 86 on a Sunday at 11 am, which is about as early as some people can manage. (If you are on the dole, life often does not begin until mid-day and 'Pebble Mill at One' becomes the breakfast TV for the unemployed of Anfield.)

We meet at No. 86 since, being one of the old Victorian town houses, it probably has the largest room. At the time of writing, the Fellowship is about 40 strong and usually 25 to 30 of us get together on a Sunday.

Seats are arranged in a circle so that everyone feels involved. A pattern of worship has emerged which we believe allows people of our local culture to fit in without embarrassment. We avoid identifiable 'orders of service' because people come from different traditions and it is important that no one feels threatened, be they Catholic or Protestant in background. Usually, two of the leaders of the Fellowship are responsible for worship—one to hold the meeting together and decide when it is right to pray, or praise, or preach, and the other to give what he believes to be God's message to the meeting. Preaching is not a monologue and folk will often interrupt with questions, comments, or to share something which they believe to be relevant. There is no hiding in pulpits or behind lecterns which would give the impression of superior status.

An important part of any worship, be it on a Sunday at No. 86, or during the week in other homes, is 'share time'.

This point in the meeting is an opportunity for anyone in the meeting to share any experience of that week which they feel is important. If someone has been to a conference, or led an act of worship somewhere else, it is helpful to let those who were not there know what went on. If someone has got a job (a rare occurrence in Liverpool), or witnessed to a friend or a neighbour about Jesus, or experienced some act of the Spirit in challenging or healing, all these and much more are important to share so that everyone can feel part of a family in praying or praising God for his love and care. It is a bit like the wife who asks her husband if he has had a good day at work—sharing is a family experience.

Singing is usually accompanied by guitar as we only have one person in the Fellowship, John, who can play piano and he is now in college training for full-time Christian ministry. Most of the songs we sing are choruses, for two reasons. Firstly, most choruses are short and easy to remember, especially if you cannot read too well. Secondly, being tied to a hymn book limits the freshness of worship. Even the Psalms encourage us to occasionally 'Sing a new song unto the Lord' (Psalm 96:1). We feel that music needs to be alive and fresh, otherwise folk can so easily get settled into a rut in which it is easy to become stale.

Prayer is always informal; sometimes someone is asked to lead in prayer, at other times prayer requests are made either for individuals or situations and then there is an opportunity for anyone to participate as they feel led of the Holy Spirit. We have seen amazing things happen in response to prayer, as on the night Julie prayed specifically for two of her friends to become Christians. That was on the Wednesday evening, at one of our home group Bible Studies; by Sunday she was telling us how the very next day, one of the friends had informed her that she was going to start going to her local church. The other one, Nadine, came with Julie to Anfield Road that Sunday, and gave her heart to Jesus the following Wednesday.

Then there was the Sunday (I was away preaching at a

church in Darwen) when my youngest son, ten-year-old Merfyn, requested prayers for laryngitis. He had been away the week before to Cub camp, in Llangollen, and had done so much talking and shouting that he had lost his voice. Two of the elders prayed for him and his voice was restored to normal. When I came home I was not sure whether to laugh or cry, as Merfyn is the noisiest member of our household!

Perhaps the most humbling experience of prayer came through Gareth, our oldest son. Gareth had been suffering from a verruca on his foot for some weeks. Tina, my wife, had given him plasters and ointment to put on it and had changed them each morning. After six weeks it was not getting any better, so almost in desperation Tina and my cousin Wendy, who also lives at 86 Anfield Road, decided to pray for Gareth's verruca. The following morning Tina asked to see Gareth's foot—so complete was the healing that she thought Gareth was messing about and told him to show her his other foot! Only after he had done so did she realise that God really had heard and answered prayer. But it made us realise that we should look to God our Father right from the start and not just as a last resort, no matter how small the issue might seem to us.

Three elders

Leadership has developed through the Fellowship's quite natural acceptance of particular people's gifts and calling. You cannot enforce Christian leadership as though it has the same authority as an Act of Parliament. It has to be earned and recognised. We now have three elders including myself, all accepted by the Fellowship on the same biblical basis: each leader has felt a genuine call from God into leadership (Acts 26:16–18); each leader has been approved by God's people at Anfield Road (Acts 6:3 and I Timothy 3:7); and each leader has received the authority of God's Holy Spirit (Acts 6:6; I Timothy 4:14; II Timothy 1:6).

At first, I was the only leader, apart from some help we received from Harry, an elder in another fellowship, who stepped back as soon as local leadership developed. As time went by some of our young men—John, Andy and Graham in particular—began to show signs of leadership and spiritual authority and were encouraged to lead worship, preach, and teach in some of the Bible studies. Not all were an instant success, but then again, how many people learn to walk without taking a few falls at the beginning?

Just as we were beginning to appreciate their leadership, things began to happen. First, Andy felt called to gain experience of another area and went to a Birmingham Baptist Church on the 'Time for God' scheme, and then John was asked to go as an assistant to a church in London. It seemed as though our heavenly Father was taking the carpet out from underneath our feet. Then along came Simon and his wife Bridget. Simon had grown up into leadership in my previous fellowship at the Rock Church, and had been a part of the leadership training programme which we ran there. Now he was available and felt right to respond to the call 'Come over and help us' (Acts 16:9).

Simon and Bridget joined us and living at the other end of Anfield Road made them very quickly a part of our community. It was only a matter of a few months before a few of the Fellowship suggested Simon should become an elder, and as this seemed good to us all and to the Holy Spirit, one Sunday we all joined in the laying-on of hands (we all joined hands and those at each end laid a hand on Simon) and he was ordained into eldership.

How Robbie, our other elder, came to join us is a much more involved story. Like Simon, Robbie had been a member of the leadership group in our previous fellowship, and had in fact been an elder at the Rock Church, but after we (the Caves) had moved on to Anfield Road, Robbie felt moved of the Spirit to go with his wife Yvonne and daughter

Dawn to help out with a United Reformed Church just down the road. Then, as he was unemployed, he had the chance of a job in Bradford, West Yorkshire and grabbed it, beginning to travel to Bradford every Monday morning and returning home on Friday evening for the weekend. Even this fitted in, as he was working just down the road from a church I had pastored some years ago and members there were able to provide mid-week accommodation for him.

It was during this time that Robbie and his family began to worship with us, on a temporary basis. The crunch came when he was offered a council house in Yorkshire. It was only then, through much prayer and heart-searching, that Robbie and Yvonne realised that God wanted them to remain in Liverpool and they felt it right to join Anfield Road Fellowship. This conviction was borne out by our Fellowship, and Robbie was recognised as the third leader in our group. He is now back on the dole, and does occasional painting and decorating jobs—but as a committed Christian he declares any extra income and it is deducted from his unemployment benefit. Not an easy thing to do where so many of those who are unemployed use this as a means of making extra money to alleviate some of the harshness of life in the inner city.

Andy returned from his experience in Birmingham and went on to act as assistant to a minister of two churches in a suburban area of South Liverpool for a further nine months. A couple of months ago Andy was married to Debbie and they are now back in the community, living just off Anfield Road. Andy has been accepted for training as a minister of the URC from September 1986.

Anfield Road Fellowship, although it is an independent fellowship, has now been accepted as an 'Associate Fellowship' of the United Reformed Church. We have a representative on its councils, with a voice but no vote. We are continuing to seek good relationships with other denominational groups and most of those in our Fellowship who lead our worship have been involved preaching in churches around the North of England—everything from Church of England, Methodist, Baptist, URC and house churches, to Pentecostal churches. Members of our Fellowship are regularly asked to be involved in conferences, both national and local, as well as consultations in urban issues, and to give testimony. We have a policy that no one goes to take part in meetings without someone else going to provide support, and in order to avoid the temptation of exaggeration.

It is important that our local members are involved in the wider work of God's kingdom as it prevents us from becoming self-centred or introverted in our vision or our mission. Visits from Christians in other countries help us to maintain a perspective and we have been privileged to receive visitors from the USA, Australia, Brazil, Nicaragua, El Salvador, France and Spain, as well as a number of people from all around the British Isles. I feel this has been helpful to many of our Fellowship, nearly all local Scousers, in having a real sense of dignity and a feeling of belonging in what can often be a very tough and threatening environment.

Youth Evangelism

An important part of our work is with local 'street kids' ie those who hang around streets corners with nowhere to go. There is no local youth club facility and even if there were, most of them would be 'turned out' fairly speedily. When they hang around street corners, local residents call the police and they are moved on—but where to? Everybody wants to complain but nobody seems to want to care. So we started a Friday night 'open house' at No. 86. Others of our Fellowship invite small groups into their homes, but Friday night is 'their night' on Anfield Road. In pile teenagers (mainly 15–19 year olds) who are drug users, car thieves, street fighters and just ordinary kids who are unemployed (Youth Training Schemes excepted) and bored. Only the 'Four S's' prevail—no smoking in the house, no swearing, stealing or spitting. Amazingly, these are accepted and often there is an apology if the odd expletive slips out. There is no pressure brought to bear; Friday night is run by members of the Fellowship but not as a club. It is a place to come, to sit and talk, or have a game of pool amongst people who will accept, care and show interest in you. Sometimes up to forty teenagers arrive between seven and ten on Friday evenings.

The snooker table which is used on Fridays, as well as the rest of the week, is one of God's 'little miracles'. Like many of the old Victorian houses, No. 86 has a cellar. We wanted to make maximum use of the house, so, three-and-a-half tons of concrete later we had a damp-sealed downstairs room which was ideal for a three-quarter-size snooker table. Just one problem we did not have the money for a snooker table. Then I received a phone call from an administrator of the Ford Motor Company's Trust Fund, on another matter. Just as an aside, he asked if we needed anything. My heart in my mouth, I mentioned the snooker table, and he replied quite casually, 'Drop me a line, with a quote.' About a month later we received a cheque and the snooker table was duly installed (after we had knocked down one corner of a wall to get it in!) 'My God will meet all your needs' (Philippians 4:19).

Being involved with the young people of the area means doing things about the problems and pressures they come under: visiting them in prison, giving a character reference in court, or helping them to come off drugs. One main task we took upon ourselves was to try to break down some of the barriers between young people and the police. 'Busy baiting' is a local pastime (Busy is the local slang word for police). The youngsters' idea is to get the police to chase them down the streets and back entries. Meanwhile, their mates come up behind and turn the police car over. On the other side, some of the police allegedly use questionable tactics in dealing with some of the young people, like making them take their shoes off (to prevent them running away), or putting them against a wall, spreading their legs, then bringing a truncheon sharply up between the legs. It is hardly surprising that there is no love lost between the two factions.

First, we showed a video film called *The Mean Machine*—an American film about a group of prisoners who used the system to beat 'the screws' at their own game. Then we invited some of our lads to come with us to a local police forum. (These were set up following Lord Scarman's report on the riots in Brixton, Bristol and Toxteth.) At first they were a bit hesitant, then they realised they had a voice, and that the senior police officers present were listening to them. It has not resolved all the problems, but it has been a real beginning.

But as well as helping and supporting the youngsters in our area, we feel we have a responsibility to share the good news with them—after all, how can they know unless they have someone to tell them? (Romans 10:14). The question was, how to tell them; traditional forms of evangelism were likely to fail and it was important to communicate with local teenagers on their own wavelength.

As they spend a fair amount of time listening to pop music, we found a Christian rock group prepared to come and spend a week playing in schools, youth clubs and church halls. In November 1983 'The Reps' came. Their final concert drew around 400 young people and over 30 stayed on afterwards to discover more about Jesus, including three of the local gang leaders, all in their late teens.

Some of them are still coming to terms with the kingdom, but it is not easy to find churches where they are readily accepted. We try to find a group of Christians, close to where those who respond live, to give them full support. We are more interested in kids for the kingdom than in building up our own little 'holy huddle', and this attitude has begun to affect our relationship with other local churches in a very positive way. Initially, some of them were very suspicious of us and felt threatened in case we began to draw members of their congregations away. When this did not happen (we are more interested in those who are not yet Christians—and there are still plenty to go around!), the ministers and leaders began to warm to us and to our work.

One example of this was an approach from a local vicar asking us to be involved in another youth mission, with 10 other churches, including Anglicans, Methodists, and Baptists. Anfield Road Fellowship was asked to share its experience of working with street kids and ran seven training sessions for about 40 Christian leaders. Another Christian rock group—The Predators—came for a week's mission in March 1985. One particular gang of older lads followed them from one venue to the next. They were not among the 29 who made a commitment to follow Jesus, but it will not be too long before they do.

What is important is that local Christians are learning to share the good news in a way that is relevant to the youngsters in the streets. At the time of writing, plans are in hand for another visit from The Predators, and this time we will be making a videotape to be used as a regular tool of mission.

Another means of evangelism offered itself just a few hundred yards up the road, at the Liverpool Football Club, at the visit of Dr Billy Graham. It was inevitable that Anfield Road Fellowship would be involved. Night after night the ground was filled to capacity and the singing was so powerful that people could hear the hymns and choruses in the pubs, in the bath and even above the TV! Nearly every single member of our fellowship was involved in one way or another—counselling, stewarding, follow-up team, even making sandwiches to feed 150 staff working at the ground on one occasion. It also gave us the opportunity of visiting over 1,000 homes around us, in order to invite people along to hear Dr Graham, and to introduce ourselves at the same time. It was a great time for bringing Christians together for giving us the opportunity to be a part of the wider church of Jesus Christ in a positive way.

Links with Other Fellowships

Since we began, a form of 'twinning' arrangement has developed between us and a URC church in Tiverton, Devon, as well as an Anglican church in St Albans, Herts. On the initiative and at the invitation of the Tiverton church, some of our members went down to Devon in autumn 1983 to share in their family weekend on the theme of 'All you need is love'. This led to the forming of a relationship between a rural church and one on the urban scene.

Earlier in 1985, 17 Tivertonians came up to Anfield to share with us in a family weekend on the theme of 'Bridge over troubled waters'. Newsletters and prayer letters are exchanged, and some of the people from Anfield have had the opportunity to holiday in the west country as a result.

The St Albans connection came through Frontier Youth Trust's 21st anniversary conference at Swanwick. We at Anfield Road had been asked to lead the worship as a fellowship—something which we and many others present found moving. At the Swanwick conference centre, Tina began to talk with one of the folk in her group, Ken, a new Christian from St Albans. It was not long before a group from St Albans came up to Liverpool. 'It looks just like London after the blitz,' said one of them after visiting the city centre. Then an invitation for 11 of us to visit St Albans followed, during which time we went sightseeing locally and in London, and spent time together in ministry and fellowship.

We greatly value our links with different churches, not just for friendship and enjoyment, but for the opportunities of learning to appreciate and understand each other's backgrounds and a rich variety of Christian experience.

Hope in the City

Another development of recent months has been the Diners' Club. So many of our members are unemployed that a lot of people have too much time on their hands during the day and experience a great deal of loneliness and boredom. The desire for companionship and fellowship has evolved into our own diners' club, when a group of (mainly) men club together to cook and eat lunch together each weekday, taking it in terms to shop, cook (invariably chips), and wash up, with a game of pool to finish off. This informal meeting fulfils a real need and helps people to feel they belong, and are important.

There are so many things to tell, but space does not permit. The fellowship is increasingly involved with young people with problems of drug abuse, ranging from those who get their kicks by drinking large amounts of cough medicine, to the more serious problem of heroin—readily and cheaply available on the streets. It is heartbreaking to see the promise of young lives destroyed by addiction, and the associated crime of the twilight world of drugs. We believe that only God's power can be sufficient, not just to achieve physical and emotional withdrawal, but that only his love can give hope and courage to face a drug-free life in a not-ideal environment. It would be all too easy to slip into negative feelings of despair and failure, but we have always to remember the promise of Jesus that he brings us abundant life, and to be a living demonstration to those around us, no matter how many times we may stumble and fall on the way.

Even in the midst of material poverty and deprivation, we continually praise God for all the evidence of his power at work. We hope that you can rejoice with us at the richness and closeness of being part of God's family, that we experience in a city where most people are hardened by circumstance and environment.

Chapter 5

Tayside Christian Fellowship

1981

Harry Pope

Tayside Christian Fellowship was founded in 1981 when several Christians in Perth felt called by God to establish an independent evangelical church in the city. Located near a shopping centre between residential and urban areas, Tayside Christian Fellowship serves the Perth inner city.

What began as a small group of 20 has grown to an average Sunday attendance of 120 in five years. Its pastor, Mr Harry Pope, was formerly manager of physiotherapy services for Perth and Kinross but has now taken early retirement to devote himself to full-time ministry.

The city of Perth is pleasantly situated at a convenient bridging point on the River Tay. It has a rich history which can be traced back to medieval times, but it is more commonly known nowadays for its whisky and insurance.

Ecclesiastically things have changed, too, since the days of the Black, Grey and White Friars. The Reformation has left its mark and the Church of Scotland is well established.

Three years ago it had 11 places of worship within the city. Now, however, as a result of amalgamation, it has only nine, and there is the possibility that this number will be further reduced.

Other denominations are also represented. These include Roman Catholics, Episcopalians, Methodists, Congregationalists, Baptists, Brethren and Salvationists. The United Free, the Free, and the Nazarene churches also have a witness in the city.

Ecumenism is gaining momentum. The Perth Council of Churches is a lively body which has been remarkably well supported by Christian churches of various persuasions. Its gatherings are normally well attended. In December, 1984, it convened a carol service in the city hall and had a capacity audience of 1,500.

Perth Evangelical Council was formed in 1980, after the Luis Palau Crusade. It conducts an annual convention and invites evangelical preachers with a nation-wide reputation. The Council, sadly, has little support from the established churches within the city, and represents only a minority of the Christian community.

So much for the social and spiritual character of this relatively small city with 42,000 inhabitants. Why was it considered to be a suitable venue for another church, and what did this church have to offer which was not already being provided?

Independent

Tayside Christian Fellowship (TCF) was different in that it was completely independent. From the outset its members resisted any denominational affiliation. They recognised only one fellowship, the body of Christ; they owned no other authority save the lordship of Christ.

The committed company who first gathered in April 1981 did so in response to requests from several different quarters in Perth. Harry Pope was approached by a number of individuals who (independently) had all come to believe that it was the right time to establish an independent evangelical church in Perth.

The numbers were few at first—fewer than 20—but what they lacked in quantity, they made up for in quality. Those who joined had come from various denominations—Baptist, Brethren, and Church of Scotland—but they were united in faith and love. Some had come through painful experiences in other churches but they were neither bitter nor divisive. They soon adopted as their theme tune, 'A new commandment I give unto you, that you love one another . . .' This chorus was frequently raised at their fellowship gatherings, and it was sung from the heart. From those small beginnings has grown a fellowship of over 100 members, a group of Christians who play an active role in the Perth Evangelical Council and who enjoy wide-ranging and good relations with other churches in the area.

The question of spiritual leadership was resolved before the church came into being. Since Mr Pope had been a lay preacher for 40 years, he was asked to co-ordinate the work and sustain the ministry. He had a professional job in the city, but he undertook to preach at the Sunday services and to exercise a pastoral responsibility. At that time there were not the personnel to justify a full-time pastor, nor was there the finance to support one. It is difficult to see how the venture could have been embarked upon without an arrangement of this type.

Elders, too, were required. According to the constitution the church would be governed by a body of spiritual men. Two evenings were spent in a study of the Scriptures, discovering what God had to say about the character, duties and appointment of such individuals. Finally it was agreed that those who were being called by the Holy Spirit should meet in a certain place at a given time. Five of them gathered, and that company has been increased as the church has grown. It was recently decided that church members should play their part in the nomination of elders. Accordingly, seven appointments were made in keeping with the wishes of the fellowship.

The work of these elders consists of pastoral care and visitation, and decision-making at the monthly meetings. At times they have witnessed dramatic answers to prayer. In one instance, the elders were called to anoint and lay hands with prayer upon Sandy Robertson, who was suffering from a severe form of cancer. After treatment that brought no improvement, Sandy was asked to give permission for radical surgery. Before he returned to the hospital to give it, the elders were called. None of the men would describe himself as charismatic, yet all are open to the leading of the Holy Spirit, and on this occasion the Lord intervened directly and healed Sandy completely. When he went back to the hospital he received further treatment and was declared to be free of cancer. Regular checks for the past two years have revealed no recurrence of the disease!

The Church Building

Accommodation is frequently a problem for a newly-formed church. Ideally it should have a building of its own in the interests of identity and credibility, but this is not generally possible when finances are limited. Struggling companies have resorted to schools, libraries, or other public places, but such arrangements are only suitable as a short-term expediency.

At Tayside a hall was rented. It was dilapidated and dirty, but it had the advantage of being in the city centre, adjacent to a public car park. It belonged to the district council, and the main tenants were the Roman Catholics who sub-let the property to various organisations. The 'Taysiders' took a lease of the building for Sunday use, but they had hardly settled in their new surroundings when the hall was put up for sale. By the end of July they were property owners, in possession of St Stephen's Hall which had been purchased for £25,000. A friendly banker loaned the cash (protesting all the while that he could not understand why he was doing it!), a Christian solicitor did the conveyancing, and an architect with family interests agreed to supervise the reconstruction.

So began the laborious process of transforming a disreputable hall into an attractive church. The work was done largely with voluntary labour. Men and women toiled incessantly for 15 months to produce a quality building that would be for the glory of God. Stone was used for an extension coffee lounge; facing bricks lined a large foyer; the wood facings were finished in mahogany. A lesser hall, attractive cloakroom/toilets, a modern kitchen and a vestry were all part of the new scheme, and the end result was a well proportioned church that was pleasing in every respect.

Actually achieving this finished building was not easy—though certainly exciting. At one point the funds had run out and the members had gathered to pray. Their prayers were earnest. How was the church to go forward? A knock on the door in the middle of the prayers surprised everyone. A neighbour from across the road had taken in a letter that the postman could not deliver to the church because there was, as yet, no letter box; she had seen the lights and wondered if the letter might be important. Sure enough, this special delivery was an immediate answer to the prayers. Someone had sent a cheque for £5,000 towards the new building!

The restoration was completed by April 1983 and the building was officially dedicated by Mr Ernest Childs of Eastbourne. It was now valued at £160,000, and much of the finance had been subscribed by members who gave sacrificially, and by interested friends who were a source of constant support. One Christian gentleman donated a total of £15,000, while an evangelical trust gave a similar amount. Those who planned to contribute regularly were encouraged to covenant. This provided a very substantial source of additional revenue. At the time of writing a final payment is being made to clear the church's indebtedness to the bank. This leaves a debt of £1,000, the balance of a personal loan which was advanced free of interest.

Increase in Membership

Taysiders are quite uninhibited in their approach to publicity. A city that is set on a hill cannot (and should not) be hid. They have a church notice board which is both colourful and striking; they have a weekly advertisement in 'Church Notices' which is distinctive and attractive; they issue illustrated invitation cards as a means of personal introduction. But one particular publicity venture was a complete flop. In 1983 it was decided that the time had come to visit every home in the city. A colourful brochure was prepared which was intended to be friendly and informative . . . definitely not 'preachy'. It incorporated a tear-off portion for enquiries and it contained an invitation to hear the Rev G. B. Duncan, the guest speaker at that time. It was even calculated that a response of half of one per cent would plunge the church into a revival, so extra stewards were briefed to cope with the influx of newcomers. Well, it did not happen. Disappointed organisers had to learn that God gives the increase. Spiritual success cannot be manipulated by over-confident workers; there is no penny-in-the-slot solution to church development.

Why did people start coming to TCF, then? In a city where church membership is declining and church doors are closing, why has the official membership grown from 20 to 100 within the space of four years? 'Taysiders' would like to think that there is an awareness of the reality of the power of God in their midst. It is hoped that visitors will worship God, saying, 'Truly God is with you.' Those who are seeking spiritual reality are attracted to a church like this.

There is a spirit, too, of loving care, which is demonstrated in a number of ways. Visitors are noticed and their names are frequently announced. If their addresses are obtainable, details are noted and a follow-up visit may be arranged. Birthday gifts are a regular feature at the family service; plants or daffodils are distributed on Mother's Day; provision vouchers are donated to the elderly at Christmas time. It is all part of the process of caring and sharing which is an essential feature of church life.

Practical and Spiritual Help

Social concern has developed spontaneously rather than deliberately, and it has many aspects. Marital problems, so much a pattern of present-day living, encroach upon the church. Men of experience are called upon to render counsel and give practical assistance. Frequently, as confidants, they cannot share the problems, so they carry burdens which are heavy to bear, and they labour for long hours striving for reconciliation or understanding. Tayside, in its short experience, has known the trauma of separation leading to possible divorce.

Unemployment is a social evil which has been tackled by the fellowship. A church meeting was called with a view to rendering practical help, but little progress was made. It was recognised that those who were out of work fell into different categories and had varying skills. There was talk of establishing an unemployment agency, or even setting up a company which would employ its own labour. As far as Tayside was concerned, the latter idea seemed like using a sledge hammer to crack a nut, so the suggestion was dropped as being impractical. Support and advice continue to be administered at a personal level. In some cases the church helps families with money management and the paying off of debts. In others, if a private business has failed, the church provides individuals with the support necessary for them to pick up the reins again.

When a spiritual healer becomes known for his social concern he suddenly finds himself in an expanding business. For one Taysider, scarcely a week goes by without his being called to deal with some human crisis or another . . . alcoholism, wife-beating, depression, sickness, broken relationships; all facets in the changing pattern of daily living.

There is a deep spiritual burden in Tayside for a residential home where the elderly can be looked after in a spirit of Christian love. Such a project would make economic sense if a number of individuals were willing to capitalise the undertaking to the extent of £200,000. Much more provision will be required for the care of the elderly than is being made at the moment, so there is scope in this field for Christian professionals with initiative and vision. It is something we are still praying for and working towards.

Ministry

Of the early New Testament church, it is said that they devoted themselves to the apostles' teaching and to the fellowship, to the breaking of bread and to prayer (Acts 2:42). As far as its ministry is concerned, TCF seeks to follow in the apostolic tradition. There are no gimmicks, or excesses, or extremes, but the word of God is ministered in the power of the Spirit, and the gifts of the church are exercised in the liberty of the Spirit. The Fellowship would not be regarded as being charismatic in the accepted sense, but if hands are raised in worship or clapped in time with the music it would not be regarded as being the end of the world!

Bible teaching follows certain consecutive themes, to sustain continuity of interest and to get the congregation involved in preparation. For example, the letters to the seven churches (Revelation 2 and 3) are being studied at the family service. Those who attend are encouraged to read a particular letter once a day for a week. A teenager will recite the letter from memory at the service, and the sermon which follows will be based on the same lesson. In this way the whole week's activity becomes a preparation for the worship on the Sunday morning.

On Sunday evening the All-Age Bible School is held. Young people contribute appropriate musical items and the Bible is taught for 35 minutes. In Perth, most of the churches have abandoned the idea of an evening service, so it is encouraging to see the numbers who gather for a straightforward exposition of the scriptures.

The word of God is expounded, but not in any cold academic sense. The truth is explained and then applied in a topical way, and in such a fashion that it meets the needs of the company. Illustrations are frequently used, taken from real life: the preacher often gives examples from personal incidents relating to the past week. In the providence of God, almost invariably a contemporary problem which has been affecting the church is discovered in the text and is expanded in the sermon. Perhaps one brother has quarrelled with another, for example, and the sermon focuses on Matthew 5:24 ('Be reconciled to your brother'); a reconciliation follows as a direct result of the preaching. So it is that the message often has a prophetic content. A word from God is communicated through his servant to a waiting people.

A new feature is the introduction of a special weekend once a month. Guest preachers from any part of the United Kingdom are invited to minister on the Saturday evening and at the Sunday services. A year's programme has been prepared, featuring such speakers as Graham Loader, Peter Maiden, Archie Naismith, Allan Nute, Keith Skelton and Peter Kimber. A brochure is being published with photographs, biographical details and information about regular services. The publicity will be distributed to members, adherents and other interested churches. It is hoped that the church will become a venue for monthly rallies; this is seen as a way of serving the body of Christ in neighbouring congregations.

Baptism and communion are regarded as important in the life of the Fellowship. The church teaches and practises adult baptism by immersion, and it expects its members to subscribe to this doctrine. The situation has raised problems for mature Christians who were baptised in infancy; but a good number of people have now been baptised as adults in accordance with this church's interpretation of Scripture. Over a period of four years there have been 50 baptisms altogether. (Newcomers have arrived from other places rather than from other local churches; in fact the church has consciously discouraged transfer from nearby churches so that they will not be seen to be 'sheep-stealing'.)

Communion is celebrated once a week, after the family service. There is a short break of 15 minutes, just enough to effect a change-over from one service to the other. With this arrangement there is no time for an informal chat with those who attend the first service, so there has been occasional discussion about altering the schedule. The Communion Service is simple, devoid of ritual or ceremony. It consists of a brief period of open worship when the Lord's death is remembered in a spirit of liberty.

Prayer is a feature of the Wednesday mid-week fellowship, which is attended by 30 or 40 people. Both men and women are free to participate. At Tayside long prayers are unpopular and 'preaching' prayers are out of the question. Those who take part are encouraged to be pointed and topical. Prayer sessions should not be boring, nor should they be a test of endurance.

During the same evening there is a time for Bible study or ministry. Once a month there is a missionary report. The evening is rounded off with refreshments and chat, while members stand around the foyer, enjoying fellowship.

Some fellowships organise a series of housegroups as alternatives or additions to a united gathering in the church.

These have been successful as a means of personalising Bible study and prayer. It has been argued that they encourage more involvement at an individual level, and they act as a spur to those who might be tempted to have a night off. These are all valid points, but they must be set against the possible disadvantages. Do they spread the spiritual resources of the church too thinly? Are they divisive in their character? Do they intrude upon the pattern of church-going? Does a group of 10 create the same atmosphere as a company of 40 or more? There is much that can be said on both sides, so it is dangerous to form general conclusions. What does well in one church is not necessarily a recipe for success in another.

The proper use of spiritual gifts is a subject which has occupied the TCF leadership from time to time. In what sense does regular, arranged ministry by one man militate against the development of ability on the part of others? To what extent should the church be an experimental training ground to determine the skills of would-be preachers? Two principles have been applied during these deliberations. Firstly, there should be scope for exercising a public gift, but not at the expense of over-taxing the patience of the listeners. There are some mature men in Tayside who are perfectly capable of sustaining a half hour's ministry session. They are called upon to participate in this way, periodically. There are others who are encouraged to develop by being asked to introduce a Bible study with a 10-minute introductory talk.

Secondly, there should be some form of in-service training providing instruction in a workshop when there can be a critical analysis of preaching style without offence. Indeed, can any church claim to be encouraging a lay ministry if it does not provide this form of tuition? It has been tried at Tayside. Notes were issued; tapes were used; experiments were conducted; homework was done . . . all with a view to intelligent exegesis and acceptable presentation. Within a few weeks there was a noticeable improvement in public speaking. This will be repeated from time to time, perhaps in a more intensive form.

TCF has a choir with 35 members of all ages and with varying vocal skills. The only musical accompaniment at the moment is the piano, but it is hoped that there will be some limited orchestral backing in the near future. As its repertoire increases the choir will be used on a monthly basis to provide a feature at the family service. It is a regular attraction on all special occasions, and it receives invitations to perform in other churches. It plans to produce a Christmas cantata each year.

The young people are catered for at every stage in their development. There is a crèche and a Sunday School at the time of the family service. For the first 25 minutes everyone meets in the main church sanctuary. Then the children disperse to various parts of the building, according to their ages. The Covenanters have a fellowship gathering after the Sunday evening service and an activity on the Friday evening. The young adults meet in various homes once a fortnight to enjoy a relaxed evening together, and they are currently becoming involved in planning a Sunday School for one of the city's outlying districts.

A word, now, about pastoral care. In principle, the elders are intended to act as shepherds to the flock, and this has always been the policy at TCF. Four 'parishes' were identified and two elders were designated for each. In theory this would concentrate the mind and heighten the awareness of responsibility. In practice it was not a resounding success, as every elder will readily admit. Care was unsystematic and sporadic.

A pastoral assistant was appointed for the year, 1984/85. He was a 22-year-old youth who is preparing for missionary work and had graduated with honours in linguistics at Edinburgh University. His weekly programme was co-ordinated with that of the honorary pastor, so visitation became more regular and more sustained.

Experience has shown that a church with 150 members

or adherents requires a constant visitation schedule occupying at least four afternoons a week. To meet this need the honorary pastor is planning an early retirement. He will have a pension and he may also receive a remuneration from the church. He has led the Fellowship since its inception and has been its regular preacher during that period.

It must be said that a venture of this spiritual magnitude brings its sorrows as well as its joys. New converts have lapsed; some others have fallen away; grievous wounds have been inflicted; slanderous words have been spoken. On one occasion a family from a non-evangelical background professed faith after attending the church for a while. The family then enthusiastically sought baptism. Sadly, they later lapsed, like the seed that sprouted quickly but then withered away. The reasons for their leaving were never fully defined.

But what about the joys? They are too numerous to spell out, but it has to be recorded that three lives, in particular, have been touched by the hand of God. In 1984, Nigel Fletcher, a young man of 24, gave up his studies in civil engineering to undertake full-time Christian work with Teenranch, Scotland. In September, 1985, Paul Wilson, the pastoral assistant, went off to All Nations College, preparing for what he sees as his life's work with Wycliffe Bible Translators. And what about Ann Whittet? She went to spend a holiday in Elie, Fife, in 1981. She and two of her family attended Scripture Union beach services and were won for the Lord. They were directed to TCF, where they have been ever since. Ann, in her 40s, with a grown up family, has just taken herself to the Bible Training Institute in Glasgow, where she plans to spend two years taking the diploma course.

God is at work in Perth!

Chapter 6

Newtown Church
1977
Brian Downward

Set in one of the largest rural areas in Britain, Newtown Assemblies of God church serves wide outlying areas and small villages in mid Wales. Originally meeting in an old upstairs room in Newtown, with 60 people attending, the church now serves 250 people from a spacious, modern building.

Brian Downward, who was until recently pastor, was trained as a state registered male nurse but later felt called to attend the Assemblies of God Bible College. Subsequently he and his wife, José, worked with Teen Challenge in New York. They then spent three years at Newtown, travelled as youth evangelists for two years, pastored an Assemblies of God church in South Africa, and finally returned to Newtown after an absence of five years. The church is now led by Alan Hewitt, as the Downwards have moved to Bournemouth to pioneer a new church there.

Brian enjoys reading and plays golf, a game which gives him the opportunity both for counselling others and for relaxing.

Newtown is situated in the very heart of Wales. Much is

known about the valleys in the south and the historic north, but mid-Wales, one of the largest rural areas in the country, has yet been of little significance in the minds of ordinary people. There are many more sheep than people, hills than houses, fields than factories. Newtown, consistent with the rest of Wales, can boast of its many churches, yet very little spiritual life has emanated from this community over the centuries; and even the 1904 Welsh Revival completely bypassed the town.

When the Newtown Church first commenced in the late 1950s, the local population was only around 5,000 people and this did not alter until the late 1960s when the Development Board for Rural Wales began to invest in its growth. It has risen in this present day to between 10,000–11,000 people. Most church leaders would consider this too small a community to establish a thriving church, but the positive attitude of its leadership was different: we may have a small town but we have a big God!

The church started with a few local people who had attended a campaign conducted by the evangelist Howell Harris in nearby Llandrindod Wells. The only accommodation they could afford was a small tent, which gave way to a wooden hut; then followed an upper room which could accommodate up to 60 people. A very loyal and devoted group consistently and faithfully served God, adding one or two here and there over the years to its numbers.

In 1966 Brian and José Downward, in their early 20s, returned from serving God in New York with David Wilkerson's Teen Challenge Drug Rehabilitation Centre; a holiday in Wales became for them an invitation to pastor the little upstairs gathering in Newtown, where their first congregation was 20 people. It was a dramatic change: from New York, with its ten million people, to Newtown with its five thousand! During those first two years in Newtown there was little harvest and few results, though the Downwards did initiate the vision to build a new church. This was obviously not the time, however, for the harvest that was to follow after their time away.

The Downwards had been invited to evangelise the youth of the nation on behalf of the National Youth Council of Assemblies of God. Their work for the Council culminated in two years of ministry in Johannesburg, South Africa. Whilst they enjoyed a most fruitful harvest there, the Lord persuaded them to return to Newtown and recommence what God had given them to do. Many lucrative incentives were placed before them to stay in South Africa; but the call to return was so clear that they felt they must in obedience act upon it.

On arriving back in Britain they were faced with the fact that Newtown already had its minister. John Redley, in his early 40s, was caring for the little congregation. However, within a matter of weeks they heard that John Redley had suffered a heart attack and had gone to be with Christ. This led to an immediate invitation from the people for them to return to pastor. Very little had changed during the years; though there was some increase in numbers, the people were still meeting in the same upstairs room. It is generally accepted that to pastor the same church twice is not a formula for success but God's grace is sufficient to disprove our formulae! Within a matter of weeks the people were challenged in their thinking about more suitable facilities vital if there was to be growth. The local people viewed the fellowship with suspicion and contempt because of its venue; they met, in fact, in a room which had once been a mortuary! Brian preached under a leaking roof; the woodwork was full of dry rot, and fungus grew on the walls. Although to the believer any place becomes a sanctuary when Christians come together to worship, the outsider generally does not take a church seriously when it meets up a flight of stairs in a decaying building!

The development of the building

It was not an easy task to convince some people of the necessity and desirability of erecting a first-class building, but without this little would have been accomplished. They were soon to learn that all lands scheduled for building and development within the town were purchased and owned by the local authority, the Development Board for Rural Wales. Personal applications were made, but each time there was a negative response. Persistently the church continued to apply until out of frustration they were told yet once more, 'There is no land, so we cannot provide you any; therefore if you go out and find some, come back and tell us, and you can have it!' This presented Brian with a challenge he could not resist.

The very next day he and José began to search the area. The first road they felt led to walk down was one of the main roads, a gateway into the town. Right opposite the high school with its 1,500 pupils, in a prime elevated position, they discovered an acre of unused land. Feeling convinced that this was where God wanted them, ideally located between the old town and the new development, they went to enquire at the offices of the Development Board for Rural Wales. 'Sorry', the Board told the Downwards, 'this is not our land but agricultural' and they gave them the name of the farmer who owned the land.

Hastily the Downwards drove out to make enquiries of the farmer. After much deliberation it was discovered that some years previously the land had (after all) been purchased by the Development Board for Rural Wales. Once more it was back to their offices. And after searching their files the Board discovered this was so, to their utter amazement. As directed, the Downwards had searched for the land and, with the promise that they could have it once they found it, they now claimed it.

A Christian architect was employed and the site excavated, but before one brick appeared above ground, all finance was spent. The people began to give, bleeding themselves dry of what little they possessed; but still there was an enormous financial mountain to climb. As yet they were unable to arrange any finance from the banks or from any other body.

One Sunday night the need was presented to the people once again. Unbeknown to them, a total stranger to the town was visiting the area; he had sat unrecognised through the evening service. Whilst greeting the people at the back of the hall, the pastor was approached by this anonymous visitor, who voiced his amazement that such a small company of people could attempt such an enormous project. 'How are you going to finance it?' he asked. 'By faith, which is all we possess' was the reply. 'I might be able to help you then,' the stranger said. This man was on holiday in the area, and he and Brian met to talk. He gave £28,000, one-third of the total cost of the building in 1977! What a relief! From then on the church never looked back. This gift opened the doors to necessary bank loans, and a loan from the property trust of the Assemblies of God was also granted.

A beautifully appointed building, delightfully furnished, was completed within 12 months of ground-breaking. On 10 September 1977, in the Year of Jubilee, 500 people, most of them visitors, marched four abreast through the streets from the old upstairs room in Wesley Street to the glorious new sanctuary on Dolfor Road. Accompanied by a police escort and followed by the media and the press, the procession halted the town for an hour. The leading dignitaries from mid-Wales joined the church in the great celebration. That day 1,000 people from all over the nation packed into the church and sang, 'I will enter His gates with thanksgiving in my heart; I will enter His courts with praise.' Overnight Newtown Church caught the attention of this vast rural area; everyone now knew of its existence, especially as endless interviews and articles were demanded of the leaders. Best of all, the congregation rose by 50 percent between leaving the old and entering the new building. People were coming to know Christ weekly, and suddenly from a small beginning the church was finding large structures emerging.

The church was open six-and-a-half days a week for administration and many day-time activities to meet the demands of the growing church. With an eye to the future, the Downwards made enquiries at the Development Board for Rural Wales as to a further acre of ground bordering on the present property. This, they were told, was the interest of various speculators; but after the church convinced the Board of the need to extend its parking facilities, the Board agreed to let the church acquire it. It was then observed that a further half-acre of land was also part of the same lot, so the church approached the Board again, this time with a view to erecting a church manse. This request was also granted, so two-and-a-half acres in all now belonged to the church.

Beyond this lay another two-and-a-half acres which, though not all suitable for building purposes, would have completed a delightful complex for the local church. So an extra four acres was granted in principle. All that Brian had to do now was to convince the people to move ahead with God in faith.

A meeting was called for the Thursday night of that week of all those committed to the work. Only a small handful of men associated with these negotiations for the land knew anything about the vision. Brian began to seek the Lord for confirmation to reinforce his plans for the future. Would the people rise to it or draw back in fear as to the immensity of the vision? Or would they be enabled through these plans to go forward in their ministry?

On Wednesday, just 24 hours before the meeting, Brian was interrupted as he prayed in the church office by a knock on the door. In walked our friend who had generously blessed the church just 18 months before. He immediately greeted Brian with the question: 'Have you got any projects on?' 'Have I got any projects on!' Brian replied, 'Come with me.' He then led the visitor through acres of brambles and nettles and thistles; the two of them viewed the land before them. 'All right, let's go back to the office and have a cup of coffee,' said the visitor. There he told of his incredible experience. Whilst on holiday in Austria, the Lord had challenged him regarding his attitude to stewardship. He felt constrained to return to England and make the journey to Newtown to ask if there were any projects, and with great joy to him and much relief to Brian, he gave a further gift of £50,000 (today's value, £120,000). He did all of this just 24 hours before the meeting of the people.

The following night the church members were presented with the enormous project but kept totally in the dark regarding the previous day's gift of £50,000. When asked if they would be willing to step out in faith and trust God, a typical mid-Wales silence broke out. To an observer from another part of the country this would have appeared to be an overwhelming vote of apathy.

But then one spoke out: 'We have proved God once; let's do it again.' Another said, 'Let's trust God and pursue the vision.' 'Are we thinking big enough?' was someone else's response. Faith was rising all over the building amongst the people.

This was the moment to inform them of God's marvellous means of provision the day before. To this the people responded by praising, laughing, weeping, all at the same time; they all went home buoyant and elated at what God had done. Brian often recalls that—had the people lacked the faith—the gift would have been returned. For without faith it is impossible to please God, and we must be willing to do the impossible without the wherewithal.

This became one of the great principles on which the church sought to build the kingdom of God in mid-Wales. Adequate finance is vital when seeking to build a strong, healthy church. Unless God had led so miraculously, unless God had so miraculously supplied, there would never have been the modern, functional building that was to prove to be one of the keys to success. People could see that they were serious and sincere; these attitudes therefore gave the church a new-found status in the locality.

Within five years of opening the church everything was fully paid for, with a little over to commence whatever new projects God would lead the church into. They had learned never to be embarrassed to ask for money, but that it is absolutely vital that they have something worthwhile to present before others. Beyond normal tithes and offerings, they discovered, folk rarely give to undesignated funds; but if there is an exciting programme to reach people and glorify God, then the saints will rise to great liberality. They learned, too, that it was vital, whilst they trusted God for their own needs, that they remain generous in their giving to others. Tithing on their income as a church was where they began, but even over and beyond this they remained sensitive to missionary giving.

One of their interests was a struggling assembly down the road in Welshpool, where a substantial building was required, as well as pastoral oversight. In this they have been able to assist, for two years providing a full-time minister, and at the same time guiding and directing the members into the renovation of a redundant Methodist church. A feeling that they were not raised up just to cater for the needs of Newtown alone, but to reach out into the villages and hamlets throughout the area meant evangelising where no recognised witness was found—this through literature, open-air services and short-term evangelistic crusades. Subsequently families travelled as far as 40 miles three times a week to enjoy the vibrant worship, teaching and fellowship. The ultimate goal was to establish where possible local mid-week groups who would then avail themselves of Sunday celebrations in the central church.

Though a very high percentage of the growth was the result of unchurched people finding Christ, there were those who joined out of the traditional churches in the area. This inevitably caused some insecurity and suspicion, but the main monthly celebrations held in the church attracted ministers and people from a wide spectrum. This helped to allay fears and doubts in the minds of other ministers, with whom good relationships were formed.

The Essential Elements

The keys to church growth in Newtown have been: firstly, the excellent facility, which became an attraction in itself; secondly, consecutive exposition of the Word, when practical teaching was given on a systematic basis, generating a great hunger for the scriptures and establishing maturity within the believer; thirdly, strong leadership, which would not allow negative attitudes to hold back the vision, encouraged and developed faith within the hearts of the people to believe for impossibilities. This leadership consists of a Senior Pastor, with two or three other fully accredited ministers making up the pastoral team. There are other men functioning as elders and deacons: these men are considered loyal, consistent and godly, men who never fail to support the pastoral leadership. Besides these, there are heads of departments specialising in youth, children, literature, visitation, senior citizens and administration, with their teams of helpers. In fact one could number up to 25 distinct ministries within the local church, catering for a wide circle of needs. Of course there always has to be someone with ultimate responsibility, and too much honour cannot be accorded to the people who supported the ministry and leadership.

The family is the fourth factor of church growth in Newtown; it has proved to be the basis of the fellowship; the church has aimed and catered for each age group, particularly in the services. Not being content with seeing Mum and Dad and all the children twice on a Sunday, they have given strong encouragement to bring all the children to mid-week services, thus establishing in their minds the importance and desirability of corporate fellowship, the church being the centre of their spiritual and social life; church is where friends and activities are to be found. Parents automatically bring their children from babes in arms right through to teenagers.

Services cater for every age group; as little departmentalisation as possible is used. Children are not 'to be seen but not heard'; they play an important role in worship, so much so that it is often children who encourage their parents to go to church, and not vice versa. Church is vital; church is fun, they have discovered. God gave an outstanding children's worker who, with her team, has poured much love into the children's lives. Today she is, along with many other duties, caring for needy children from divided homes, within a building partly provided by the church. The church has discovered how vital it is to establish in very early life good routines and habits in attending the house of God.

The fifth key to church growth in Newtown is the number of ministries that involve such a great percentage of the people. Wherever people are willing to be used, then a function in the body is found for them, from cleaning the church to running a full-time literature work. One example would be the Bible and book ministry, which began in a tiny store in the market place, and developed into a six-day-a-week retail outlet and a travelling shop, which visits a different market place each day. This vision was realised by a young man wonderfully converted, who, within two years, turned his back upon a lucrative agricultural business and by faith began to do the work of the Lord. Though the church has given him no regular financial support because he wanted to rely directly on God, the fellowship has benefited immensely from his ministry. The church encourages people to branch out in whatever work God is giving them, and wherever possible make it self-financing, and yet still function under the umbrella of the local church. It has been found important for people to be free to serve the Lord independently and yet submit to God-given leadership within the local assembly. Where this formula has been acknowledged, God has abundantly blessed the work.

Other areas of ministry are the teaching and training courses held at Pentrenant Hall, Churchstoke. An 18th century manor house was purchased by Brian Downward and Peter Rees. Beautifully restored and furnished, it lies in five acres of land overlooking delightful countryside. Here each year men are trained for pioneering new churches in the United Kingdom under the auspices of the Assemblies of God Home Missions Department. Young people also receive short-term training before going on to serve in local churches. The course is sponsored by the National Youth Council of the Assemblies of God; since youth groups also use the facilities for retreats and seminars, the centre provides an exciting ministry which blesses the local church and receives a return. This centre is now totally in the hands of Peter Rees and his family. These are just two examples of the many ministries functioning in the body which make up a vital witness both locally and nationally.

'Get involved' is the motto of the church. Wherever a growing church is to be found, problems will also be there; a change inevitably brings unrest. People feel secure within their proven structure. Hardly, if ever, does this apply to new converts or young people, but inevitably some who have been on the way for many years. Sadly there were those whom nothing would ever please, who gave no encouragement and showed no enthusiasm, who remained sitting on the fence watching whether success or failure would come out of each attempt to build for God.

Building for God does not only mean creating structures, buildings and visions, but also expressions of worship and fellowship. In Ezra we read of the laying of the foundations of the new Temple, and of all those who had returned from bondage, young in age and experience, who rejoiced and celebrated with all their hearts. Bondage was all that they had known and experienced; there was therefore nothing to compare with the new life and the Temple, so they were determined to enjoy every blessing. There were, however, the ancient men who could remember Solomon's Temple in all its glory, and therefore they could not find it in their heart to show any enthusiasm for this new day; they wept and mourned whilst the others praised and worshipped.

The experience at Newtown was similar, as a new wave of liberty and freedom swept through the assembly. What power and blessing came into their presence, and all who were new in God (and many veterans, too) enjoyed it, though some of the old 'wineskins' creaked under the strain of receiving the new wine. Yet within whatever context the assembly found itself as God moved the people onward and forward, resistance to change could not be allowed to stifle the life which comes from God. The church cannot be run on sentimentality or democracy, but on reality; and therefore, though painful and sometimes costly, advance it must. Occasionally individuals were lost to the fellowship, and this brought sadness; yet it was soon learned that sometimes we have to lose a few to gain many. Dead branches fall away in order that new ones may grow in their place and produce fruit as pruned by God's Spirit.

Living for God in a small rural town also brings difficulties. In a community where small events and scandals take on enormous magnitude, one has to accept this fact, with no means of escape. Being a leader in a small town singles you out in the community. People either love or hate you, and if the latter applies, then you can become the subject of the gossip that fills the town's narrow existence. (This smallness can, however, work for good, as a church can make a big impact in a small community.)

Having served God for 13 years in mid-Wales, just when everything is secure and viable, Brian and José Downward and their family have been called away by God to commence pioneering all over again in Bournemouth, a town where they are unknown, with no building to inherit, and little or no finance at their disposal. Just as they are looking for financial security and a settled way of life for their three children, God has pulled up their roots and transplanted them elsewhere. Even in this new venture the fellowship at Newtown seeks to be involved: a branch is going over the wall to bless others. A few individuals have been released with Newtown's blessing to stand with the Downwards in the work. If only something of what God has done in Newtown can go with them, then great things will be accomplished. The big God of a small town can do big things still as they attempt big things for God in a large town.

On the Downwards' leaving Wales, God has provided a most honourable and gifted leader for the assembly. A great handover day took place in May 1985 as Alan Hewitt and his family took over the responsibility for the church. This will inevitably lead to change and further development, but one thing is certain: the church in Newtown will glorify God.

Chapter 7

The Isca Christian Fellowship

1967

Jack Hardwidge

ISCA Christian Fellowship has grown from 150 members in 1980 to 350 in 1985. Located in Exeter, this network of house churches is spread throughout the city and environs, drawing its members from inner city and suburban districts.

Jack Hardwidge, a former college lecturer in maths, heads the group of four ministers, two full-time and two part-time, which also includes Bob Whitchurch, Norman Alford, and Tony Wade. Jack is married and enjoys gardening and entomology.

'Isca' is the old Roman name for Exeter. The city has a population of about 100,000 and, by reputation, has for many years had some spiritual life. The Isca Christian Fellowship is a 'house church', owning no church buildings and regarding the areas where its people live as its 'parish', (but not to the exclusion of anyone else).

The main leadership is pastoral: Bob Whitchurch taught history until 1981, and since then has served the church full-time; Norman Alford is a director in a local firm of outfitters; Tony Wade is a manager with SW Gas; and the team is led by Jack Hardwidge, who taught mathematics until becoming full-time in 1974.

There is an associated church at Exmouth—Ichthus Christian Fellowship—led by Howard Govier, a solicitor, and another associated church in mid Devon, called the Taw Vale Community Church, which is led by Clifford Bennett, a buyer in the animal foods industry.

Total Sunday congregations approach 500 with about 350 committed members.

Origins

On 11 October 1966, my wife Daisy and I bought at auction a large house in Pinhoe, a village just inside the boundaries of Exeter. Here we made our home and it was here that the Fellowship met during its infant years.

For 25 years we had been active members of a Brethren church in another part of the city and, for the last 15 of these years, had been praying for revival, like many others up and down the land. Arthur Wallis, who at that time lived 10 miles away, led us in this intercession as we met to pray in his house once a month, and he led us into the baptism in the Spirit. By the end of these 15 years of intercession the charismatic renewal was breaking out all around us.

However, in 1964, misunderstandings in our church about the Holy Spirit led to difficulties, and we eventually felt obliged to pull out. This was in June 1966, and by the end of the year we had moved away from the area to the house in Pinhoe.

There was no intention, at first, of establishing a church. It was a time of much confusion. We had neither gathered a group together nor had any specific idea of direction—we simply thought of praying and worshipping with our family and the few others who had joined us. However, right from the start we did resolve to be free from mere traditions. We were really very much on our own, apart from Arthur Wallis (who was a tremendous help to us, but who had his own group in his home village of Talaton), and various travelling charismatic speakers. These speakers helped us greatly in our weakness, and we owe them a great deal, but they did produce a few cross-winds of instruction. We did not follow every suggestion—we have always been a little independent! Eventually we started doing the teaching ourselves.

In the earliest days we ran a boys' club in the house yet always felt we would concentrate our efforts on more mature age groups when the Lord gave us opportunity. So when students began to come to us from Exeter's many colleges, we abandoned the boys' club, which had yielded little fruit, and began to concentrate on adults. Down through the years many students who have come to the university or other colleges, have joined us, stayed on, found a job, married and settled down. Bob and Muriel Whitchurch came to us like this. So we met in our home in Pinhoe until we could not accommodate any more people. Every available space in our lounge was occupied every Sunday morning and when the stairs began to fill as well, we moved to a school-hall in Exeter. At that time we numbered about 80 people.

A couple of churches in Exeter were critical of us and some of the residents in Pinhoe were originally suspicious. One local lady looked in at the gate to say that she did not agree with all that went on in our house! But she was unable to say what it was she disagreed with! Who knows what stories circulated in the village! However, we never answered back and have tried to maintain a loving attitude to them all. We have, very occasionally, joined some of the churches for communion, when invited. So we have lived the criticism down during our 18 years of existence. Anyway most of the Christians in Exeter were probably unaware of our existence at first.

In later years people have asked us why we started something new. 'Why do you not bring your enthusiasm and life into existing churches?' they ask. The answer is that this was what we had been trying to do in our original church, but our efforts were resisted. Two churches in Exeter did kindly offer us fellowship but they had their own problems about the Holy Spirit and the need for 'new wineskins' anyway.

Housegroups

After a few years our mid-week prayer meeting had grown and we considered dividing it. We hesitated, fearing that we might drift apart and lose our unity. The Lord showed us however, that if we kept the leaders together we would keep the whole church together. So we divided the prayer meeting and our leaders began to meet together regularly. The prayer meetings developed into our present housegroups and our housegroup leaders have met once a week since then. This has maintained our love and unity.

Later we realised that our housegroups were really following the early church pattern in Acts 2, engaging in 'fellowship, apostles teaching, breaking of bread and prayers. Only later did we realise that God was establishing 'housegroups' in many other churches and looking back we can see that he has often done the same thing in the past in various times of spiritual awakening.

Our people are committed to a specific group. Usually it is the nearest to their own home, but for newcomers, existing relationships sometimes dictate which group they should join. In the groups, which average 15 members, deep friendships are forged and people care for one another.

The housegroups are the backbone of the fellowship. Each congregation is really a gathering of the housegroups which comprise it. We keep no membership roll but reckon that those who are committed to the groups are members of the

Isca Christian Fellowship. In turn, the leaders of the housegroups commit themselves to serve the people under their care. There is no 'club' type of membership—people have to come regularly and be involved to be counted in. We do not keep new converts waiting to join a group. After all 3,000 were added to the church at Pentecost on the same day, so we get people involved right away.

The housegroup leader is the pastor of the group and in this his wife stands with him. Thus the total pastoral load in the whole fellowship is shared by many, according to the Moses/Jethro principle of Exodus 18.

The leader's relationship to his group could more truthfully be likened to a father caring for his family than a general directing his troops or a teacher instructing his class. He sees that his people are fed by Bible study and that they develop their relationship with the Lord and each other as they worship and pray together. He cares for them and encourages them in outreach. If necessary he guards the group from those who might disrupt. He is concerned with each individual's progress and aims at 'love, which comes from a pure heart and a good conscience and a sincere faith' (I Timothy 1:5).

It is in the housegroups that people's gifts begin to develop. Leading the discussions, praise or prayer is a task shared out to brothers and sisters who have the necessary gift. In particular, the housegroup leader encourages another man, who will lead half of the group when it divides. All our leadership arises from within like this; we have not imported any leadership; there is no democratic process and leaders are not elected. Rather, when their gift becomes apparent to all, this is recognised by the existing leadership and they are appointed, along with their wives, with prayer and the laying-on of hands. So we believe the Lord chooses them. We aim at theocracy rather than democracy!

Here, if I may be permitted a personal view, I think our housegroup leaders and their wives, are the finest bunch of men and women in the world!

One final word about the role of housegroups—they play a part in evangelism. Sometimes people bring in unconverted friends. Sarah was a member of the local babysitting rota where she met Gill and brought her to the group. Gill had deep depressive problems, but after some weeks was born again and set free from evil spirits. Then her husband came, saying he had a new wife! He was already a Christian and finally her son joined too and soon entered the kingdom. In another instance, Bill, a divorced, lonely man, was brought by his son. In the course of time he, too, found the Lord. There are many other examples but none of this is achieved by turning the housegroup meeting into something evangelistic—it simply carries on normally. People who become Christians in this way have no problems adjusting to church life—they are already in, with loving relationships growing daily.

Congregations

At present we have four congregations meeting in Exeter each Sunday morning, one associated congregation at Exmouth (10 miles away) and one in mid-Devon (18 miles away). Of the four in Exeter, three are the result of multiplication of the original group. We have felt that when a congregation numbers more than 100 it needs to divide; otherwise people do not have opportunity to participate fully. Dividing has always been painful to people who really love each other, but it is a price to be paid for the expansion of the kingdom. We allocate half the housegroups to one new congregation and the rest to the other new one.

The fourth congregation was a separate fellowship under the leadership of Tony Wade, until we joined forces. Prior to this we had known each other well and shared a similar vision. In 1984 it seemed right for us to unite and we are now very much one.

The Exmouth congregation had its origins in a group

who travelled to Exeter to meet with us each Sunday. They met mid-week and on Sunday evenings in a housegroup in Exmouth and continued like this until numerous enough to hire a hall and meet in their own town on Sunday mornings. They now have two housegroups and increase by new converts. They direct their own affairs but we are still very much one in spirit.

The Taw Vale Community Church is a gathering of country people which has taken some years to establish. We were not involved in its origins but share many things at leadership level and are very close in spirit. Both of these churches join us in celebrations.

Our congregations meet in school, village or church halls. They vary in size, at the moment, from about 40 to 120 people, and comprise three to six housegroups each. The Sunday meeting consists of half an hour or so of worship, followed by teaching or breaking bread. The teaching is planned ahead but the other parts are unstructured and open for the 'body' to participate. A group of excellent musicians leads the singing but people suggest a song, lead in prayer (short prayers are favoured), read a scripture, give a testimony, speak in a tongue, interpret or prophesy, share a thought or a vision, or sing a song to the Lord for us all.

Sunday mornings are wonderful times; they are a weekly festival of praise for us. Sometimes we all sing in the Spirit, sometimes worship in silence or as the music plays. We believe it is the Spirit of God who plays the harp of God at these times, plucking each string to harmonise. Sometimes there will be prayer for healing, although most of the prayer for healing and deliverance will be in private, along the lines of James 5. This gives opportunity for confessing sins, being forgiven and, of course, forgiving all others.

Is there any leadership involved in this open worship? Yes there is! It is there if needed. The congregational leader and the housegroup leaders are present, but, while their authority is recognised, it rarely has to be used. In these meetings there is much freedom—freedom to stand or sit, to kneel or dance, to speak or be silent, but there is not freedom to spread discord or to spoil things for all the rest. After the worship, the children leave and are catered for separately.

The second part of the congregational meeting is given to breaking bread or teaching, usually on alternate Sundays. During the winter, the teaching often follows the same theme in all the congregations. In recent years we have thought through the Sermon on the Mount, the Parables and Romans. The teachers are mostly the housegroup and congregational leaders.

The rest of Sunday is unstructured—housegroups or congregations may go out together or meet in someone's house for 'group-tea', or families may just enjoy time at home. However, the young people do meet together regularly on Sunday evenings. In the winter the evening may be used for seminars for specialised groups dealing with such subjects as marriage, relationships, leadership, outreach, or general topics such as church history and biblical prophecy.

Everyone needs a close relationship with a small cell group, as well as a relationship with a wider group with a greater range of ages and gifts in the congregation, and also occasional participation in a large group for encouragement and inspiration. So we have celebrations at approximately monthly intervals. They consist of worship—perhaps the 'high praises' of our people—and teaching. The latter will sometimes be given by a visiting speaker and sometimes by our own leaders, which gives us an opportunity to share important things with the whole fellowship.

Wanting to be all together as often as possible, we organise barbecues, walks, and a raft race down the river Exe in the summer. Most of the rafts actually float, some even move faster than the river, but most people are really in for the fun and the splash.

The fellowship game is volleyball with a little cricket thrown in occasionally. For the past few years we have had an annual family camping holiday on the coast where we ride the surf, fight the tide and lick ice-cream. The kids love it and so do we all!

The year 1985 saw our first May week-end conference at Pontins in Brixham, where 350 of us assembled. Table tennis, bathing, snooker, country dancing and kids' praise parties combined with worship and teaching to make a memorable week-end of all-round fellowship.

Our treasurer, Gordon Alford, has an exceptional gift for handling our finances. We teach our people to tithe and to bring the 'tithe into the storehouse' (Malachi 3:10). Each month the finance group of about seven men, including the congregational leaders, meets to ask the Lord what he wants us to fund. We are not trying to distribute the money in hand, because the balance is usually small, but we aim to do what he directs, trusting him to provide. We have only once or twice been 'in the red' and we knew each time where we had gone wrong.

In addition to the second half of the Sunday morning meeting, when we cater separately for newborns to 10-year olds, all children have mid-week activities. We believe that the task of bringing up children in the fear of the Lord is the major responsibility, not of the church, but of the parents, and especially the fathers: 'Fathers, bring up your children in the training and instruction of the Lord' (Ephesians 6:4). What we do as a fellowship is intended to assist parents, and especially fathers, in this area. So we consult them and expect all parents to give a hand when help is needed. We appoint leaders, firmly believing that 'government' is the basis of order. Our main aim is to build friendship between the children, in peer age groups, so that they will have good relationships through the difficult years of adolescence. We do not run a Sunday school or engage in child evangelism.

While we have a 'bulge' at crèche age, we have only a relatively small number of teenagers, so catering for them is still being explored. The church is taking more responsibility for their spiritual welfare than in the case of the younger children.

Leadership

Our leadership in Exeter has developed as we have grown. The leadership of the whole church is in the hands of the four congregational leaders named in the introduction. We meet weekly and handle all matters which concern everybody. The very real love and unity which binds the four of us together necessarily influences the whole church.

We do believe that good government is essential to peace in the community. This involves clear and adequate administration, without the over-administration which stifles initiative, and a clear recognition of leadership. Our government has never been 'heavy'. We hold with Abraham Lincoln that government only needs to do for people what they cannot do for themselves!

In each of the four congregations the leadership consists of the congregational leader, plus his housegroup leaders. We try to avoid the terms 'elders' and 'deacons' (does anyone know what a 'deacon' is supposed to do anyway?) So we prefer to speak of 'leaders' in different areas—outreach leaders, leaders of children's activities, music leaders, housegroup leaders, congregational leaders.

Everywhere, everything possible is based on relationships. The four congregational leaders and their wives occasionally meet for a meal to strengthen the bond between us. In addition, each congregational leader has a special relationship with each of his housegroup leaders. They spend an hour or so together once or twice a month, sometimes with wives, and share all insights, joys, and concerns. Paul said, 'Whatever you have learned or received or heard from me, or seen in me—put it into practice' (Philippians 4:9) and 'Follow my example as I follow the example of Christ'. So we learn from each other in friendly relationships. If I had to select just one thing from among the many ingredients which have contributed to the building of this 'house of God' I would say it is the relationships between our men. Relationships run like a thread through all we do—leadership, children's activities, housegroups and evangelism.

Evangelism

Most of our growth has come from people moving into the area or from new converts. A large proportion of our people have had no Christian home background. We have few local 'transferees' because we make a point of never asking members of other churches to join us! Nor do we advertise in the press or in any other way to try to attract other Christians. Most of our converts come through local or business friendships rather than through special evangelistic activities.

However, recently the Lord has been emphasising 'outreach' to us, as he has been doing to many churches in the land. So in 1982, recognising that our leadership was mainly pastoral and that we lacked real drive and expertise in evangelism, we asked Ian Marlow to be our full-time evangelist. He had lived among us for a few years as travelling secretary for the Universities' and Colleges' Christian Fellowship in the south west. His brief was not to do it all but to 'prepare God's people for works of service' in evangelism (Ephesians 4:12).

As a result our street preaching goes something like this. It is Saturday morning; and the outreach group moves after prayer to the pedestrian precincts in the city centre. Here a sketch board is erected and someone preaches briefly, slapping on paint to illustrate his points. He then offers a handout. The rest of the group are in the crowd, ready to open up a conversation or pass on a home-produced leaflet. Sometimes, drama or music may be used.

We also visit door to door and distribute bi-monthly, in the areas where we live, *Cross Purposes*, a high quality, well-produced paper. It deals with a separate topic each time, such as 'Family under Pressure', 'Behind the Mask', 'Out of

Darkness', 'Life after Life', 'Money Makes Your World Go Round', 'A Future without Fear', 'Fit for Life', and 'Marriage Matters'. Many people read this paper, especially the life stories of our own folk. One housegroup leader received a telephone call from a man saying 'I saw your name on *Cross Purposes*—my wife and I feel there's more to life than we experience—can you come and talk to us about Christianity?' After six weeks of reading *Good News Down The Street*, they are both in the kingdom and in the church. (We heartily recommend the book *Good News Down The Street* by Michael Wooderson.)

We also have a Start Right course for new converts, running for 6 to 8 weeks, based on our own publication. It covers the teaching, death and resurrection of Jesus, water baptism, baptism in the Spirit and commitment. We encourage new converts to work through it and place them in a housegroup at the same time. Ian has spearheaded this and gathered together those among us with an evangelistic heart. He has also established our young people's fellowship, which is thriving and begins to be a training ground for future evangelists and leaders.

But still, most of our new members come by personal contacts. This is one reason why we have so few meetings for our folk. They need time to make and maintain friendship in the neighbourhood (or at college) which may ripen for the kingdom of God. Within the unity of the whole church, we encourage activities on the perimeter. Various ladies' groups meet on their own initiative and invite neighbours, some of whom have come into the kingdom this way. In fact it is our women who form most of the local relationships. Some couples use the *Jesus Then and Now* videos, inviting their friends home to watch them.

Since the start of 1985, directed by prophecy and inspired by what Roger Forster is doing in SE London, we began to pray about pioneering the kingdom in one of the Exeter housing estates, where we knew of no evangelical witness. After guidance, one congregation assumed responsibility.

Cross Purposes was distributed over a few months and then door-to-door visiting began, the congregation and the outreach team working together. We have now established a small housegroup of our own people who live there, and some interest is developing in the estate. When we have made more progress here, one of the other congregations will begin to evangelise another estate.

Relationships with Existing Churches

We regard ourselves as just a part of God's church in Exeter and our headed stationery says so. We are glad when God blesses others and do not try to compete with other churches or 'sheep-steal'. We support every city and nationwide project, like Mission England with Billy Graham, and we join with other evangelical or charismatic leaders in local fraternals. While we shoulder the main burden for our local 'All Saints' meetings, again we do not use them to advertise our own activities. Many folk from all denominations are blessed in these charismatic meetings. We discourage our people from criticising others, even if others criticise us. All this, we feel, has led to a healthy relationship with other churches in the city.

Property

The Fellowship now owns two properties—not 'churches' in the usual sense of the word. *The Salt Cellar* is our craft and coffee shop, opened in 1979. Here we sell Christian books and cards, Tear and Traid craft, crafts by local Christians, and midday lunches and teas. The coffee shop seats 25. The staff are all our own; the enterprise is very well run by the women in the fellowship. While it does not make a profit, neither does it drain the church finances. The fellowship owns the freehold and our own limited company runs the shop. We aim to meet non-Christians and local church people here and to show how kingdom people can serve others. It is a fruitful place—better for us than any 'church' building! We have also recently acquired a property we call *The Cornerstone*, which provides two large rooms for youth groups, teaching seminars, musicians' meetings, and many other things.

Leadership Relationships

For many years we have taken the view that the major responsibility for our people lies at our own door. The leaders here are those who will have to give account (Hebrews 13:17). But we have also asked for and received advice from men of God in all denominations and shall continue to do so. But in recent years, Barney Coombs has been a special blessing to us. If I had to define the relationship it is this: Barney, at my request, is my personal pastor. Our relationship is based on warm friendship. When he visits us, his encouragement builds us up and his wise counsel is a gift from God to us all. If we face a particularly difficult problem, he is only a 'phone call away. It is through him that we have been able to learn from such teachers as Bob Mumford and Charles Simpson, and it was he who sent Vic Gledhill to teach us about deliverance. Meeting with the many church leaders with whom he is involved has continually inspired us and widened our understanding and vision. We love him very much.

New Wineskins

In the early days of our praying for revival, long before this church was born, I heard, along with others, the Lord saying that new wine would need new wineskins. So when the Holy Spirit came, we knew there would be changes. I cannot help feeling grateful now that we had to leave our original church and start again from scratch. It was not what we had prayed for but it did mean that we could abandon old traditions. We hope, now, that we do not place a premium on special buildings, Sunday clothes, or sanctimonious expressions of worship—we try to be the same all seven days of the week, kingdom people.

We want our daily work, our marriages, our families, our housegroups, our shop, our relationships, our general manner of life, all week long, to be a model of what the Lord wants his kingdom to be—naturally supernatural. We fear that a refusal to change can be a major cause of stagnation in the kingdom of God, so we teach our people that 'change is here to stay'. We do not want to settle down. 'There is much land still to be possessed' (Joshua 13:1).

Difficulties

There have been two real crises during our 18 years; they were difficult and painful. The first was in the early days, when a group left another church and joined us—somewhat under protest on their part. We lacked strong government and they caused disunity. Progress halted until, after we as leaders had cried to the Lord for help, they left us. Growth resumed and we resolved to govern better. The other occasion was more recent and was in connection with our practice of delivering people from evil spirits in the name of Jesus (Mark 16:17). Most of one housegroup left us believing that Christians could not need deliverance. But we continued to grow, and to see many people set free.

At times of crisis or anticipated crisis the Lord has often said to me, 'Why do you worry—did I not say that I would build my church?' At such times he has graciously sent us prophetic warnings when some cloud was about to rise above the horizon. So we have been able to close ranks and stand together.

The Future

We do not see any major changes in structure or aim in the immediate future. However, we do anticipate a continual forward move in evangelism into new areas and in the demonstration of accompanying miraculous signs in which we are at present lacking.

We are also beginning to think more about any overseas involvement the Lord may want from us.

We shall soon have to think about a fifth congregation in Exeter, but when the time comes, our people will be ready and willing, and the new leader will be apparent.

In the meantime, we shall pursue our aims as before, which are, in simple terms, to *evangelise*, to *care for* and to *train*, with the threads of *relationship* and *non-religious behaviour* running through all three aims.

Three Crucial Factors

There have been three crucial factors in the development of the Fellowship. First and foremost, the Holy Spirit. Churches can copy each others' external ways, sing the same songs, do the same things, but unless it is the Holy Spirit at work, nothing will be built. We believe the Spirit baptises individuals into the 'body' (1 Corinthians 12:13)—and when the 'body' operates with love and warmth, then the 'army' can begin to operate and bring people in.

Secondly, the realisation that pure, clear, loving relationships are the essence of the body of Christ. If we lose our unity, we shall cease to be blessed (Psalm 133).

Thirdly, the development and recognition of leadership among us, which is an example and which serves, governs, counsels, cares and hears God.

This church is not perfect. While we pursue an ideal, we recognise that we have to handle the actual.

We do not claim to have arrived, but we do think that we are on the way, thanks to the Father, Son and Holy Spirit.

Chapter 8

The King's Church, Aldershot

1984

Philip Greenslade

The King's Church in Aldershot is located in a suburban area that borders on an army town with a catchment area of a quarter of a million people. It has doubled in size in the last five years to a weekly attendance of about 600.

The work of the church goes on under a team led by Mike Pusey, its foundational pastor and a leader in the charismatic movement for many years, and Derek Brown, who is engaged in a wide-ranging ministry throughout Britain as well as overseas. Philip Greenslade, author of this chapter, is known for his teaching and training ministry both within and beyond the church.

All three men are married and have worked together for over ten years. Derek and Philip enjoy reading and sport while Mike is the enthusiastic chaplain of the Aldershot Football League Club.

We stood in the heavy darkness. There were six of us in the

dilapidated, damp and blacked-out former cinema. Never as a leadership had we faced such a major decision.

We sensed an unspoken agreement that God was making his decision known. Months later we stood there again, with 1,500 other Christians in a building now restored in a resplendent green. Fifteen hundred voices sang 'Majesty' to the praise of the glory of King Jesus in the new centre dedicated to him.

Our opening ceremony declared our faith in the transforming power of the grace of God. A building built for darkness was now full of light. What was designed for fantasy was now dedicated to truth. In the place where many had sought escape from reality many more would find reality. 'Escape to Victory', the last film shown at the old Odeon cinema, seemed quaintly prophetic. For the King's Church it was a new beginning.

Seventeen years earlier a small Baptist Church had gone through the usual induction formalities. After five years as pastor of Basingstoke Baptist Church, Mike Pusey was being welcomed as pastor of the Baptist work in Farnborough, at the 'unanimous' invitation of the 40 members of the church.

Already, at Basingstoke, Mike had begun to feel the impact of the emerging 'charismatic movement'. Having himself been baptised in the Holy Spirit soon after conversion, he readily associated with those leaders in main-line denominations who were also experiencing new dimensions of the Holy Spirit's life and power. Soon he began teaching on the person and work of the Holy Spirit. Encouragement was given to the exercise of spiritual gifts, and a ministry of divine healing commenced.

'Moving to Farnborough, this reputation went ahead of me,' Mike admits. With a desire in the church for decline to be reversed and a fresh impact made for Jesus, the early months seemed to confirm the picture of a church prepared to follow its new leader. Mike had made clear to the deacons how convinced he was that only the Holy Spirit could bring recovery, renewal, restoration and revival. The small membership began to take new steps of faith, including the purchase of a manse. It was agreed, Mike recalls, 'that the commencing salary would be £50 per month. This was to be increased to £60 when the average Lord's Day offering for the month reached £30! It wasn't long before the increase came into effect.'

Numbers increased too. There was a steady response to the new pastor's love and care. It was certainly proving full-time work as each of the members needed time with Mike. He taught the scriptures consistently, emphasising the fundamentals of the faith. He began to explore the word of God to understand the realms of spiritual experience as yet unknown to the church. 'I had decided,' Mike remembers, 'that every manifestation would be completely open and above board.' Friday evening prayer meetings for revival became the place where members began to sample the new wine of God's Spirit. 'We lived dangerously,' Mike recalls, 'but it was exciting as well!'

Before long a conflict came to the surface. Everyone was agreed on the truth and reliability of the Bible. But when some biblical events were shown to have application here and now, it was a much more uncomfortable matter altogether.

Some reacted so strongly that they chose to leave quickly in search of another spiritual home. Others stayed to fight it out! Others again, more bemused, stayed on in the hope that such things would soon end and the church return to a more predictable lifestyle.

Despite these difficulties the Lord began to bring people to the church who were, in Mike's words, 'hungry for God'. They came from a 20-mile radius of the church. One of the first to be saved was a teenager, Bill Rice, now the full-time evangelist on the staff of the King's Church.

Mike continued to teach and care for this growing and mixed bag of people. Corporate prayer and expectation for healing were key features. Mike stressed that the church was a family and emphasised friendship and the formation of close relationships.

This teaching was advanced through visits by gifted teachers coming to prominence in the charismatic movement: Campbell McAlpine, Arthur Wallis, Ian Cockburn, Gerald Coates and Peter Lyne were among those who helped achieve significant breakthroughs in the life of the church.

Worship began slowly to unfreeze. Meetings opened up to allow praise, prayer and spontaneous spiritual contributions. By 1974 the membership of the church had grown to 150 with an annual income of £10,000. Grace was growing too. 'The first time I walked through the door,' recalls Dave Brown, now one of the pastoral staff, then with a broken marriage, 'I felt the love; it was almost tangible.'

Two Are Better than One

Plurality is a difficult but important biblical principle, especially for church leadership. Mike had quite naturally looked for support and fellowship to a few ministerial friends who were sharing the same thrills and traumas of change. But the instinct for shared ministry went deeper. The realisation that the ministry was not a 'one-man band' came as revelation from God to many pastors in Britain during this time. Mike was one of them. He became convinced that the church would begin to measure up to the New Testament and make an impact only if other men, called and gifted by God, were drawn into the ministry alongside him. Mike made this an urgent matter of prayer. A vision began to take shape, though no-one realised where it might lead.

In 1972 Mike met Derek Brown, then working in a legal practice in a neighbouring town, but eager to serve the Lord in preaching. The two men became friends. Mike gave Derek opportunities to teach the word of God at mid-week meetings of the church. Derek differed from Mike in personality and gifts. Here was the man, Mike believed, who was the answer to his prayer. Derek's appointment to the leadership of the church in July 1974 was not without difficulty. Change is difficult for some, and opposition from a few was strong. But Derek was set apart on a full-time basis to serve alongside Mike, not as assistant pastor, but as co-pastor. He was given the freedom to develop his own particular gifts in co-operation with Mike. The seeds of plural leadership had been sown. Mike deserves great credit in all this for his openness, his obedience to the Lord, and his farsightedness.

With a broader base, the church began to have a broader vision. Derek brought an obvious 'prophetic' thrust to bear on the growing fellowship. The ministry gifts of Ephesians 4:11 began to figure frequently in the discussion. There Paul wrote, 'It was he who gave some to be apostles, some to be prophets, some to be evangelists, and some to be pastors and teachers.' Since then this dual ministry exercised by Mike and Derek has 'equipped the saints for service' and raised up other ministries in the Church.

The tension between Mike and Derek has often been acute, but by the grace of God they have held together, and as iron sharpens iron so they have sharpened each other's ministry and function in the church. Tension has itself proved creative. Here are men prepared to risk all to practise the plurality they preach. The vision of another Antioch began to clarify—a church large enough, mature enough and rich enough in the gifts of ministry to be a resource centre for a whole region and beyond. To date, three other gifted ministers and five members of pastoral staff serve with Mike and Derek, making ten in all. Others have been commissioned to serve the growing number of groups, fellowships, and churches that look towards the King's Church for help and support.

Derek recalls the days when he joined Mike in ministry in the church and remembers how he and his wife, Irene, were attracted to the pattern of the Antioch Church and its ministry as described in Acts 13:1–3, the emphasis being on the diversity of gifts and on the sending out of ministries.

Much of Derek's current work load has to do with gathering the fruits of that vision.

Further Advance: Commitment and Relationships

The steady growth of the church throughout 1974 and 1975 brought two key issues to the surface. The first was the level of commitment of those enjoying the life of the fellowship. It was time to define more clearly what was involved in joining and belonging to the church. A commitment course was drawn up to meet three immediate needs.

Firstly, the growth of the church was no longer by transfer of mature Christians from other churches. Now, the newly-converted and those never associated with a church were being added. To avoid the continual repetition of basic teaching to the same group of people, a separate programme of instruction for newcomers was obviously needed.

Secondly, by this time the majority of the members were baptised in the Holy Spirit. If this quality of life was to be maintained it was vital to provide a place where the biblical basis of the pentecostal experience could be taught and experienced. The newly-established charismatic stance of the church was thus part of the foundation.

Thirdly, the church had by now come to a shared understanding of the financial commitment involved in belonging to it, an understanding that needed to be maintained.

All existing members of the church went through the original course. Restyled, expanded to cover 12 sessions, and renamed 'Committed For Life', it still serves as the doorway into the church.

In this way we test the profession of faith made by the newly converted and look for evidence of repentance. In order not to discourage the dynamic of conversion, baptism in water can take place before the end of the course at pastoral discretion. Long-established Christians enjoy the review the course provides. After completing the course, everyone knows what is expected of him or her and can give to others a clearer picture of the lifestyle and convictions of the church.

The second major development at this time arose out of the need to maintain the quality of caring relationships between the members. In a church which by now had grown to 230 people this was becoming difficult. Housegroups were introduced to meet this need.

Careful teaching and training were given to selected couples who became house or home group leaders. The members of the church were divided among the group geographically. These groups supplied basic care and fellowship to supplement the inspiration of the larger celebration gatherings. Sometimes they emphasised friendship, at other times discipline or evangelism.

For nearly 10 years the groups served a very useful function and seemed an unchangeable part of our lives. By 1984, however, we began asking whether the new wineskin was not in danger of becoming as inflexible as the old one! Were the groups in danger of becoming stereotyped? Were we creating an echelon of leadership which was more concerned with office than with the pastoral care of the people? Were we becoming a passive people again, not releasing and using the God-given gifts among us? These questions and others prompted the decision to disband the groups at the end of 1984. At the time of writing we are considering reintroducing a looser system of pastoral care groups to cater for the desire for regular fellowship and mutual encouragement.

Divide to Multiply

By 1979 the old Baptist Chapel in Queens Road, Farnborough, offered standing room only. The decision was made to divide the fellowship into two, the members living in Cove (a distinct area of Farnborough) forming a new congregational unit alongside the orginal one. Some still recall the trauma this change brought! Separating from friends with whom we had long worshipped was painful. But with tremendous courage and some trepidation the people of God responded wholeheartedly to this drastic move. It proved decisive.

Wisely, Mike and Derek determined not to divide their loyalties by each taking responsibility for a congregation. Both would service each of the newly formed groupings. These met separately for three Sunday mornings in the month, coming together for a great celebration on the first Sunday of the month. This format proved viable and effective until the numbers celebrating outgrew the public halls available and provoked the search for a new and larger home.

God has his own ways of bringing his people together. In 1980 a group of believers in the nearby town of Fleet approached Derek for advice and counsel. With its roots in Chard, the Fleet Christian Fellowship had prospered under the leadership of Alan and Pam Robertson. Now they sensed the need for new direction and impetus. Derek spent many hours with Alan and his fellow-leaders and slowly gained their confidence and the trust of the people in their care. Eventually, the Lord gave clear guidance to the merging of the Fleet Fellowship with the Farnborough Fellowship believers who lived in the Fleet area. This was a costly move, not least for Alan Robertson himself. But Alan was brave enough to make this move and brave enough never to regret having taken the decision to be part of a bigger work of God. In this way the third congregation was born. It soon began to grow, cared for by Alan Richardson, the latest member of the full-time ministry team.

1982 was to prove a significant year for the church. A New Year promise from the Lord held out the prospect of 150 people being added in the next 12 months. Soon a further congregation was formed on a large housing estate at Pinewood.

Further afield—much further afield—in the far north east of Scotland in fact, new links of friendship and respect were forming. As a result, Mike and Margaret Pusey were commissioned to live and work on the east coast of Scotland for six months. This proved to be an important time both for them and for the churches which received them.

Back home, further unusual events were taking place. Together with their pastor, a lively group of young couples moved from a small Baptist church in a neighbouring county to help form the nucleus of yet another congregation, this time in Ash Vale. Congregations then numbering eight (since reduced to five) formed a vital link in the 'celebration–congregation–cell' approach to church nurture and growth.

At about the same time a fall-out from a local parish—unlooked for by us—brought a further influx of believers, some upset and in need of healing, all seeking to progress with God. Regular celebration evenings held in another Anglican church were significant growth points throughout the year. Clear testimonies, ministry for healing, exuberant praise, sensitive worship, and simple but direct preaching of the gospel—all combined to touch many lives for Jesus. By 31 December we were amazed and thankful to God to realise that 150 people had been added to us in 1982!

Another Faith Venture

'If you want to grow, extend the base of ministry,' say the pundits, among them the strategist who advised Yonghi Cho. So we did. We had always instinctively done this, adding to our pastoral team before, not after, the numbers demanded it. 'You provide the shepherds and I'll produce the sheep,' seemed to be the Lord's word to us. In the autumn of 1983 we took the step of faith to appoint four men to full-time pastoral ministry in the church.

The setting apart of these men, now supported by two

more, was memorable. From the large bowl of oil to hand, the new pastors were liberally anointed. Faces shone and hair glistened. It was felt then that all the people should receive the blessing, and oil flowed everywhere. Fleet Civic Hall seemed awash with it. Some suits never recovered: dry cleaners prospered: wood flooring was never better nurtured! Not so much an ordination, more a lubrication, but the Holy Spirit made his distinguishing mark on the brothers and they have proved their worth since.

By now no public building could comfortably contain all who gathered to celebrate their joy at being in God's kingdom. There was certainly no space for God to fill. Fruitless searches for a suitable venue left us drawing an unexpected and initially embarrassing conclusion. We were to buy a building of our own. 'Lord, you can't be serious?' we protested. 'The church is people, not buildings, Lord! We've preached this too often. We're supposed to be radical!' But 'Buy a building' was our unanimous understanding of the voice of the Lord. Finding one was not so easy.

Inflatable buildings were inappropriate. Land to build on was prohibitively expensive. Finally, our attention was drawn to the deserted and neglected Odeon Cinema in the centre of the neighbouring town of Aldershot. Enquiries to Rank Ltd revealed that the property was available. Our offer of £200,000 was accepted and the adventure of moving to the King's Centre was under way.

With few of our members living in Aldershot itself, we asked for volunteers to settle there. Ten families and two members of the ministry team moved into the town to form the nucleus of a new congregation and to serve the work of the Centre. Not all our judgements at this time were accurate. Moves were planned that did not materialise. Expectations were raised that were not fulfilled. Perhaps as leaders we learned not to over-define the vision.

Before our move the Lord had another surprise for us. In its recent past our name had undergone various alterations: at first 'Farnborough Baptist Church', then 'The Farnborough Christian Fellowship', and later—as our borders stretched beyond the town—'The Christian Fellowship'. Now the Lord made clear to us as leaders that names are important. Moving to the new base was a coming of age for all of us. Jesus, we were reminded, had more than fellowship in mind. He had come among us to build his church. We had quietly dropped the word 'church' several years before thinking it such an abused word as to be open to total misunderstanding. Now, he made it clear, we were to resurrect the basic New Testament term for the people of God. So we became 'The King's Church'! If anyone thought this a trivial move, we soon saw that more than a change of label was involved. Almost at once a serious case of discipline arose and we knew we were a church rather than just a fellowship!

Strengths and Weaknesses

Needless to say our strengths are sometimes our weaknesses. The pioneering spirit in the church is so strong that it often obscures a sense of history. But the King's Church stands in a strong dissenting tradition. We revere our 'forefathers' who pioneered the recovery of 'lost ground' in their own generation.

We rejoice in the knowledge that we did not begin this story and will not end it. The attitude of some radical Christians who act as if they were the first real Christians who ever lived is not for us. Nor do we presumptuously believe we shall be the last! Our links with believers across the world in traditions other than our own are growing stronger. They may have different styles but, like us, they seek to respond to what the Spirit is now saying to the churches. We desire the unity of the whole body of Christ but suspect that, given love and prayer, the recognition of the diversity of ministries described in Ephesians 4:11 is a major practical step to that end. We cherish the view that every local church has its own unique flavour. It delights us to discover that not every one is exactly like us! We hold good relationships with many churches in what is now styled 'Restorationism' without being aligned with any one of them.

We are strong in prophetic preaching, in the declaration of the present word of God to his church. Basic instruction and commitment to newcomers is also thorough and effective. But consistent pastoral teaching of the apostolic doctrine to feed the people is not so easy to find in the church's programme. Nor does our current structure of church-life allow much room for the expository preaching of Scriptures to open up the whole counsel of God. We rely on the variety of ministries that serve the church to supply this 'breadth of mind'. None of these weaknesses is necessarily permanent, nor due to lack of desire or available gift. Rather they are symptomatic of people and leadership still coming to terms with newness.

The church's influence is spreading to an ever-widening circle. This, too, exposes weaknesses. We are undoubtedly reaching many more lives for Jesus Christ, but at the inevitable expense of not being on hand, as we once were, to help shape those lives into his likeness. Perhaps inevitably, the church must become less defined and more open-ended. How to cope with this change without lowering the level of commitment so that the blessings of many begin to rest on the dedication of only a few is something we are watching carefully. For every sheep who enters the church, at least two or three are now being blessed and sent out to enrich other folds.

Ours, too, is a ministry-orientated church. This is as it should be. Church is not a spectator sport. Everyone, is called to find his or her gift and use it. Currently, we live with a certain tension between this and our original roots as a church strong in family-style relationships and body ministry. Some church members find the demands of ministry upon them too taxing for their present level of maturity; others flourish and grow in the changes.

The Lord has raised up a devoted band of intercessors, mostly ladies; recently they have been given much greater recognition and encouragement. But it is still true to say that we do not yet know as clearly as we want to how to mobilise the whole church for prayer.

Women are respected and valued highly in the church. The women of the church are attractive and outgoing. They willingly embrace balanced biblical teaching on submission and seem to flourish under it. Many of them are finding increasing fulfilment in praise, administration, evangelism, intercession, pastoral care, as well as in business and in the home.

Since we moved to the centre, the children's ministry has expanded accordingly. Led by one of the pastors, it is set to receive higher priority in our plans for the future. How best to minister to teens and older young people is a constant debating point; several new experiments are under way.

Socially the church is on new ground. It is carefully facing up to the challenge and opportunity of having a centre which is becoming a focal point in the community. In this area too we await development.

Leadership

In the last 10 years a major thrust of the church has been the encouragement of men to assume their God-given roles and responsibilities. Derek had worked with Philip Greenslade giving leadership training for several years before Phil joined the team in 1982. Successful Men's Days grew into several well received 'Towards Leadership' training programmes; a much appreciated bulletin of the same name followed, as well as a nine-month School of Ministry for men already in full-time pastoral work. Recent conferences for pastors, elders and leaders have brought between 250 and 800 men each time from all over Britain for several days of teaching and ministry.

The King's Church is ambitious–ambitious, we hope, for the Lord's glory. Its leadership has a variety of gifts that makes for healthy and creative tensions. It is a leadership which is open to question and in which no one is beyond criticism. The brotherly love shared amongst the leaders usually makes admonition palatable. The church owes a great deal to its minister of administration, Peter Gaut. The experience we have gained under his leadership has given him a base from which to be an economic adviser to an increasing number of other churches and Christian businesses. And at the 'sharp end' is our indispensable secretary, Sandy Stockwell, soon to be helped by another secretary and more modern equipment. Here we know we need the wisdom of God. We want to grow into a large and efficient church without becoming the Christian equivalent of the 'high-tech' industries all around us.

Right now, too, we are grappling with the implications of a strong challenge from an international visiting ministry to think nationally as well as locally or regionally! Since this challenge arose, a growing national organisation committed to bringing kingdom power and principles to bear on the medical profession has moved its base to the King's Church. Another well-known ministry is in the process of joining us, and with our encouragement is investigating the development of satellite broadcasting and Christian television in Britain.

We are beginning to think in European terms also, perhaps for the first time, and are looking to strengthen our links with Christians in France, Germany, Norway and elsewhere. Could it be that God is now preparing a new invasion force for the spiritual reawakening of Europe, and that British Christians will be included? On a wider front we have ministry links with New Zealand, the USA, South Africa, India, and especially Sri Lanka—all of which broaden our vision and keep us open to the worldwide body of Christ of which we are such a small part.

Our evangelist, Bill Rice, heads a keen evangelistic team, not all of whom are young people, gaining experience in open-air work, mime and drama, preaching and healing on the streets. Significantly the 'leaven' is affecting the 'whole lump', and the Holy Spirit is mobilising the whole church for evangelism by the people for the people.

What Sort of People Are We?

We are the usual mix of ordinary people serving an extraordinary God: a sergeant-medic with the Paras who served in the Falklands, an ex-porn-king and convict; several teachers, doctors and nurses; electronic experts, specialists of all kinds at the local Royal Aircraft Establishment, 'boffins' of all shapes and sizes; self-employed builders, irrigation and landscape engineers, carpenters, and plumbers; a warehouse manager of one of Britain's largest food retailers; accountants and solicitors; ex-drug addicts and the social workers who once dealt with them; travelling salesmen; shop assistants; a hospital porter, a gardener, a potter, and a postman; two traffic policemen and a policewoman; a newspaper editor and one of his reporters; men of high finance in the City, and check-out operators at the local supermarket; retired men and women and crowds of children!

Worshipping with us is seldom dull. What would you see and hear? Joyful up-tempo praise to guitar and piano accompaniment; clapping and dancing by old and young alike; uplifted arms, bowed knees, faces to the ground—whatever is scriptural and appropriate to the prompting of the Spirit; shouts of exhilaration and songs of adoration interspersed with prophetic songs, and corporate singing in the Spirit; specific prophecies brought to a microphone at the front of the auditorium; sensitive worship in which the majesty of Jesus is central.

Now 45 minutes or an hour has passed. An hour's Bible teaching usually follows with strong emphasis on doing as well as hearing. Or, on occasions, a movement of the Spirit across the body occurs to preclude further preaching. He leads some to administer healing, others to pray with brothers and sisters as tears flow and laughter rises, others to hug or comfort each other. What we are now beginning to witness leads us to believe that our prayers for God's supernatural intervention are being answered.

Our Sunday evening 'Meet The King' meetings are more

varied, sometimes more direct with special musical items and testimonies to the changing power of Jesus. There is clear preaching that calls for a definite response, and there is ministry to the sick and needy.

A newspaper reporter who had never visited us censured us as kill joys for our opposition to occult practices in the town. Another reporter from the same paper who *did* visit us called us a 'very happy bunch of people'!

Our people are lively, loyal and loving. Several visiting ministers from overseas agree that they have seldom found anywhere in the world a company of people so free and so open to the Holy Spirit. Our people are brave and flexible. They have to be, since constant change is here to stay in our church. What we lack in a sense of security is more than offset by the spirit of adventure.

'Lots of vision, strong momentum, and get-up-and-go' was the first impression of Bob Butterworth when he joined the church four years ago. 'I'd liken the church,' he says now as one of the five pastors, 'to a powerful rally car: the maps are good; the steering is sometimes wayward; and we never slow down for the corners!'

Staying the course is not easy. Miss Keeley has. Our oldest member at 97 years of age, Win has been a Baptist for 52 years and has been taught by five different ministers. Now—amidst unimaginable and sometimes unwelcome changes—she is taught by ten! Why is she still with us? 'The goodness of the Lord is the secret of my long life,' she will tell you. Why is she here in the church? 'Because the word of God is faithfully taught and I appreciate the love of the fellowship,' she answers.

As we stood recently with 1,600 others to hear evangelist Reinhard Bonnke, we anticipated the day when the King's Centre would always be as full. We sensed again, as we often do, that we have a lot to learn and that this is only the beginning. The pace is quickening in the move of God, and there are more surprises ahead. But that is another story . . . and Jesus is the author of it.

Chapter 9

New Life Church, Worthing

1911/1972

Andrew Kane

New Life Church is not so much a new church as a church made new. Set in a coastal resort traditionally noted as a place for retirement, this church is challenging and injecting new life into its environment. It has grown from 95 members in 1970 to 365 in 1985—more if one includes members from two now independent churches planted by New Life.

The senior pastor of the team is Andrew Kane, author of Let There Be Life, *who was trained first as a quantity surveyor and subsequently at Spurgeon's College, earning an honours degree in Divinity. He is married to Marilyn and has a daughter and two sons. As a writer and full-time pastor, he has little time for hobbies but enjoys sports and reading.*

'House chair' at the Baptist Spurgeon's College is a free-wheeling, rumbustious student meeting where matters great and small are discussed. The tradition is that every man settling in a church during his last year at college announces details of the settlement at house chair. Presented in a semi-serious vein, the news is greeted with a mixture of humour and goodwill.

In January 1970 I caught the chairman's eye and rose to announce my settlement. 'I'm pleased to announce that I have accepted the call to the pastorate of the Durrington Free Church in Worthing.' This brought cries such as 'Costa geriatrica!', 'Early retirement!' and 'I do like to be beside the seaside!' All good fun and designed to remove any pomposity or hypocrisy from one's approach.

The comments, however, were not entirely inappropriate. Moving to Worthing with my wife Marilyn in the summer and beginning at the church in September I discovered that the congregation could easily be likened to the popular image of the town.

The number on the membership roll was in the 90s. One wag suggested that this was also the average age so that when folk retired and joined the church the average age was lowered. There was an almost total absence of folk between the middle teens and the middle 50s. The majority consisted of retired people. The congregations numbered between 40 and 50 in the morning and around 30 in the evening, while the mid-week meeting usually raised about a dozen. This situation was emphasised when, on returning to college for the week-end refresher course some 18 months later, the fellows were trading stories of the first year in the ministry. Some were boasting of numbers of baptisms, marriages and baby dedications; my contribution was a record number of funerals.

The people, however, were warm and friendly, but there was hardly any depth of vital spiritual life. It was a cosy, sleepy, elderly community that bore little family likeness to its New Testament forebears.

The first 18 months passed with enough encouragement to keep us going but with little signs of any significant breakthrough. The key to that came when our evangelism committee sensed that our need was more for an 'inner mission' than for outreach.

Richard Green, one of the committee, had experience of God renewing other churches through his association with Barney Coombs at Basingstoke. 'I know of a man,' said Richard, 'whom God is using in this kind of ministry and he happens to live here in Worthing. His name is Campbell McAlpine. Do you think we could ask him?'

It was agreed that I should go to meet Campbell in order to discuss our thoughts about an inner mission.

Arriving at his home some days later, I was met by a short, tough man in his early 50s. With bald head, clipped moustache and strong Scottish accent, he first appeared stern. He quickly got down to business and I soon became aware of the spiritual stature of the man. Sitting there talking to him I became increasingly conscious of the superficiality of my own spiritual life, and as we began to discuss the work of the Holy Spirit in local churches today, I realised that with Campbell there could be no half measures. 'It's all got to be done God's way,' seemed to be his recurring theme. I began to wonder how we would cope with that radical approach at Durrington. God's hand was on all the arrangements however, as the only date that Campbell had available for that year was the very period we had in mind—early October.

In my heart, I really wanted the best, the very best, for the church and during that first meeting with Campbell McAlpine, I sensed that this desire was going to cost me more than I had ever dreamed. 'Revolutionise the church, Lord!' I was not sure, however, that I wanted Andrew Kane quite so revolutionised. I felt strangely inadequate, insecure, vulnerable. Before this renewal was over, God was going to graciously reshape my whole concept of the ministry; fortunately I could not see all that at the beginning.

The Turning Point

During that summer we prayed, planned, then prayed some more, as we looked towards the inner mission. At last 1 October arrived and Campbell began his ministry. Each evening he preached to between 70 and 80 of us, bringing a particularly significant message, on the raising of Lazarus, on the Wednesday.

> 'Before we can expect new life and resurrection power, we have to roll away the stone and expose what is death to the gaze of Jesus. In many lives here, there are areas of death. Dead works cluttering up our time, shaming our testimony, quenching the Spirit. Roll back the stone! Let the Lord in to deal with them!'

As Campbell preached this message, the Spirit began his work among us. However, to use the famous phrase of Joe Church of Ruanda revival fame, 'it was not the top blowing off but the bottom falling out'. The message of repentance and the call to brokenness was a new sound to many of us in the church. I had thought all that was for the unbelievers. Suddenly we were aware of God's holy ways searching our lives and exposing so much that was death in his sight. Traditions, practices, habits were now being questioned. 'What does God really want?' was the burning question.

Later in the week the theme changed from repentance towards life in the Holy Spirit. With his strongly biblical preaching, Campbell taught the need for each believer to be baptised in and filled with the Holy Spirit. Following the deep soul-searching and consequent feelings of helplessness that the previous preaching had produced, here at last was the solution. The promise of the Lord Jesus concerning the Holy Spirit seemed almost too good to be true: 'If a man is thirsty, let him come to me and drink. Whoever believes in me, as the scripture has said, streams of living water will flow from within him. By this he meant the Spirit, whom those who believed in him were later to receive (John 7:37–39). Our realisation of death had produced a burning thirst for that flow of life which was in the Spirit.

Campbell invited folk to come forward as a token of seeking the Lord Jesus who, as the baptiser in the Holy Spirit, would be the one we needed to approach. Small numbers of us came to the front, some kneeling, others standing, some seated with heads bowed. Campbell quietly moved among us and, where necessary, prayed; but the awareness at that moment was of each one coming to the Lord himself.

There was no dramatic manifestation. My longing had been for another Pentecost—the visitation of the Spirit of which I had read in the revivals—but it was not so. For me personally, the first sign was a deep experience of peace and rest; I felt I had come home. I knew an assurance of being a child of God and that God was my Father and that was enough. Looking around, I could see peace and joy and tears breaking forth on the faces of others. For some, there was immediately a new prayer language in the Spirit; for some others among us, that would come later.

A sense of thrill overwhelmed me as I sat on that front pew looking around somewhat dazed. So this was the new thing that I had been searching for these past years! This was the Holy Spirit. I suddenly realised that we were at a watershed; here was something on which we could never go back. Death was past. Life was slowly coming to the body.

You might have thought that many would have flocked forward to seek and receive the Spirit of power for the Christian life, but this was not the case. Only about 15 of us did so, but in the purposes of God it was the start that he was looking for. Smallness never seems to be a problem to God.

In the months following the inner mission, I came to realise that we now had a situation in the Church which the Reformers called *ecclesiola in ecclesia*—little church within a church. Luther and others would form a nucleus of true believers within an unbelieving church, that it might act as leaven and influence the life of the whole church for the better. Such had never been my desire but there could be no doubt that a new spiritual dynamic had been released within the old church.

This small group met fortnightly on a Tuesday evening to share their new dimension of faith, new discoveries in the Spirit and to learn to worship. Here we began to sing Scripture choruses to learn to contribute spontaneously as we responded to the leading of the Spirit, to experience the range of emotion in worship from exuberant, noisy praise to the living stillness of silence. We also experimented hesitantly and tentatively with some charismatic gifts of the Spirit. I use the word 'experimented' deliberately, for how else could we co-operate with him?

For the next 18 months or so, we lived out our church lives on two levels. In the group we learned together as we travelled to meetings, swapped books and tapes and generally stimulated and encouraged one another. In the main body of the church things remained much the same with little changing, though I did begin to teach on the person and work of the Holy Spirit.

There was little tension between the two groups: in the church everything was openly talked about and every effort made to include and welcome all. Looking back on those days with the experience of some years, I am sure that what eased away any serious tension was my presence as the minister leading the new beginning which God had made. I have counselled many from other churches who have had a renewal experience only to find that their testimony was not well received by their church leaders. This has placed them in a difficult position: should they remain in their church and seek to influence it for good? should they join others in their church with similar sympathies and become a pressure group, or would it be best for them to leave and join elsewhere where their new spiritual fervour would be welcomed?

For many in historic churches these are burning issues.

Our situation has demonstrated that it is possible for a small group to influence and bring about transformation in the larger church. Tragically this would not be true of most situations, where, all too often, the end results are splits, hurt, recriminations and bitterness. How can these be avoided and what lessons are there to learn?

I am convinced that the key to bringing the new through into the old is the attitude of the presiding minister. Where he is sympathetic, then those testifying of new life and renewal should be encouraged to co-operate fully with him and throw their energies sensitively into church life. Where a minister is unsympathetic, whether that be for theological, aesthetic, emotional or psychological reasons, it seems to me that a group within the church can do more harm than good. The Lord is as concerned for 'old church' as he is for 'new group', as he made plain in Matthew 9:17: 'Neither do men pour new wine into old wineskins. If they do, the skins will burst, the wine will run out and the wineskins will be ruined. No, they pour new wine into new wineskins, and both are preserved.'

The kingdom of God is surely big enough for all sorts of groups—it is men's hearts that are not usually big enough.

But to return to the story: how did our small group begin to shape the congregation so that a whole new church emerged? God led us to re-examine a large number of foundational principles.

Centrality of the Bible

As we experienced more of the Spirit's working, I became increasingly aware of my own limited knowledge. It was at this point, in November 1973, that God powerfully broke in to point out the important next stage. I was to write to certain men who had experience of charismatic renewal and were also reputed Bible teachers and invite them to take a teaching week-end for the whole church in Durrington. The names and subjects came quickly to mind.

Campbell McAlpine returned in March 1974 and spoke about renewal in the knowledge of God. This teaching ensured that we were kept on course in the centre of God's purposes and not blown on to the shoals and reefs by preoccupation with secondary matters. God himself was to be our objective and Campbell guided us, by the power of the Spirit, in the right direction.

Other speakers came at roughly two-monthly intervals, through to the summer of the following year. These week-ends included Friday evening, two sessions on the Saturday and the Sunday services. We had teaching, teaching and more teaching. The Spirit gave tremendous authority to what they said; their teaching, backed up by personal experience, gave the word of God fresh vitality. As a result of this most intensive period of teaching we realised afresh that the Bible has to be an essential part of the new foundation that God was building for our lives.

I use the phrase 'new foundation' deliberately and carefully. My whole church background had been conservative evangelical, which had given me a real love for the Bible and an appreciation of its centrality in matters of faith and conduct. For years I had listened to teaching in Brethren, Baptist and Reformed churches, hearing countless sermons. Now, through this experience of the Spirit's renewal, a subtle but significant change was emerging in my understanding of Scripture. There was about them a new authority; the word had about it a new insistence. Passages pressed themselves forward demanding to be taken seriously and actually acted upon, put into practice, now.

I realised with some dismay that, for whatever reason, whether I or my theological school had been at fault, I had known little of the Bible's authority before. The practice of splitting the word of God into past, present and future sections had been as undermining as the rewriting job done by liberal interpreters. Many a time I had heard the phrase,

'Oh that's not for today,' until it coloured the whole Bible. In fact the Spirit began to insist, 'This *is* for today. Will you believe it and put it into practice?!' I think it was David Pawson speaking of the Bible in relationship to his church in Guildford who said, 'I want nothing in this church which is not in this book. However, I do want everything that is in this book in this church.' This was exactly the position I was coming to.

Let me hasten to stress that I did not throw away all the help in understanding the Bible provided by scholars over the years. The well proven principles of biblical interpretation and exegesis must hold good. What I sensed happened was a releasing of the Bible to be the word of God with all authority in the present: that has got to be one of the primary matters of restoration for an individual and local church.

The Need for Vision

As the group read, travelled, visited conferences and heard teaching from many sources, a new perspective on the local church began to form in my understanding. God has always revealed his desires to his servants the prophets, who could then instruct and lead the people: 'Write down the revelation and make it plain on tablets so that whoever reads it may run with it' (Habbakuk 2:2). Clearly God wants his people to be able to move swiftly and efficiently as they identify all that he is doing in the world.

All these things came together towards the end of 1974, and at the beginning of the new year 1975 I declared as a prophet this vision to the people. It consisted of all that the Lord was wanting for us, as I understood him, in our local expression of his church today. It was based on the work of his Spirit that we could observe as he moved in many places around the world. Yet it was not just a copying of what others were doing. This vision was born from much prayer, and I believe it was God's plan for us in Durrington.

The influence of the teaching week-ends had been profound, but they did not immediately transform the scene. The church as a whole was more interested, more informed, grateful for some of the blessings of renewal but hesitant about personal involvement. By now, among those of us in the group there was a growing conviction that the blessings we had received were not just personal. We longed that everyone in the church might come to know the joy of life in the Spirit. I was also by now convinced that what God wanted was a radically different corporate lifestyle for the church.

It was in that situation that I took the bull by the horns and declared to all the people the nature of the church that we would be. God had shown me that we were to be a church knowing the dominance of Jesus and filled with Christians who were alive in their faith. We were to have a proper structure and system of oversight, a living organism rather than a mere set of committees within a sterile institution. As a living community of God's people we were to embody the truth of ministry, to exercise spiritual gifts, and to involve all members. From a strong emphasis on the Christian home we were to reach out in a wider ministry that would encompass others.

Starting early in 1975 I worked through each point of the vision. On each occasion I carefully avoided teaching systematic doctrines. I sensed that God was wanting me to make each point a specific prophetic declaration. In effect, I was like Ezekiel before the valley of the dry bones commanding that life should emerge and that the body should take form in a particular way; in other words, I wanted to speak God's creative word into the situation to bring about change, not to dwell on general principles.

I freely confess that it was far from easy. It would have been so much easier to teach the principles and to allow the people to decide for themselves on specific issues. At this time, however, it was necessary for the way ahead to be clearly charted and declared without debate. This was the way we were going. This was what God wanted. And if that sounds arrogant, I can only confess that I do believe God gave me no option. I personally believe that there comes a time in the development of every church where the issues must be declared with authority from the word of God under the anointing of the Holy Spirit.

It is at this point that one is invariably asked, particularly by pastors, 'And did you lose anyone through doing this?' The answer is yes, we did lose people. In looking at the lists I calculate that some 19 people came off the membership-roll over this crucial period. In addition to that, there were probably up to another dozen who were technically members, but who were unable to identify with us through the changes. There is a great deal of sadness that anyone felt it necessary to leave, although the majority went amicably with good personal relationships being continued. One or two, it has to be acknowledged, left in bitterness, which was doubly sad.

Anyone with a pastor's heart will know the pain of this. We sense it in Jesus himself: 'From this time many of his disciples turned back and no longer followed him. "You do not want to leave too, do you?" Jesus asked the Twelve' (John 6:66–67). Did Jesus need reassurance at that point? Whatever his feelings about those who had left, he clearly felt it necessary to reach out for a definite affirmation from the others. Vision is essential for a people who desire to venture forward in faith. Sadly, the very clarifying of it brings a dividing of the ways.

The vision became our manifesto, the accepted guidelines for the future development of the fellowship. Since that time parts of it have been fulfilled. Other parts have been modified or amplified in the light of our growing experience of the Spirit. Then again, new areas altogether have opened up which have enlarged the vision. Many a time we have found comfort in God's word to Habakkuk following the declaring of the vision in his day: 'For the revelation awaits an appointed time; it speaks of the end and will not prove false. Though it linger, wait for it; it will certainly come and will not delay. See, he is puffed up; his desires are not upright—but the righteous will live by his faith.'

The Releasing of the Body

The heart of this new vision for the local church lies in the phrase 'the body of Christ'. Of all the descriptions of the church in the New Testament it is this one which is most pregnant with meaning. As the apostle Paul wrestles with language to convey his revelation of the church it is to this picture that he returns time and again. In his great epistles the truth rings out, 'Now you are the body of Christ and individually members of it' (1 Corinthians 12:27).

Many books on the church in the past two decades have highlighted this truth. Significantly when Michael Harper wrote one of the first booklets on the charismatic movement in this country he entitled it 'Power for the Body of Christ': focus was no longer on a personal experience of the Holy Spirit, important as that is, but on the church.

The Church Growth school of studies has exercised an important and influential rôle over recent years. These scholars carefully analyse growing churches. They have found common features in these churches irrespective of where they are located. Peter Wagner in his book entitled *Your Church Can Grow* (Gospel Light Publications: Glendale, California, p. 71) puts the understanding of the local church functioning as a body high on the list. In his chapter 'Let's join laymen's lib!' he writes, 'Every single believer has been fitted into the body of Christ according to God's master plan and has been given one or more spiritual gifts to fulfil that function properly.' This he calls 'laymen's lib': 'As far as church growth is concerned laymen's lib has opened up fantastic new possibilities. If laypeople became excited about what they can do for God and their church, the sky is the limit.'

Seeing folk discover their areas of giftedness and begin to move with increasing confidence in their ministry has been a great joy. We all need to feel significant to feel that our contribution is equally important. People's hearts, loyalties and commitments are drawn out when they feel personally involved in their church and are not merely spectators at the performance of the professionals or the few.

Thus we have seen ministries evolve in the creative arts: music, composition, art, drama, banners; ministries to do with caring: counselling groups, care groups, playgroups, luncheon clubs; ministries specialising in evangelism; a full-time evangelist has been appointed to coordinate evangelistic supper parties, open air work, prison ministry, door-to-door visitation.

A people who are alive in God and actively involved will then draw others because they are enthusiastic and attractive, so 'the whole body . . . grows and builds itself up in love, as each part does its work' (Ephesians 4:16).

We are thankful to God for the fruit of our church's ministry: two churches planted from us, each having now grown to about 100 adult members; our church presently having a membership approaching 400 most of whom came through conversion; seven full-time staff and a financial budget well in excess of £100,000 per annum; children's and youth ministries among up to 600 young people each week. Such a list however would lead to a wrong conclusion, for it might give the impression that we had somehow arrived. The fact is that we face as many challenges and difficulties today as we ever have and are more dependent on God's grace and wisdom than at any time.

Working a new concept and experience of church life into an established church is a long and testing commitment. We human beings are strangely stubborn, resistant to change. Even when new life begins to bear fruit, it is often viewed with caution. Each new phase is accompanied by resistance and even loss of those members who can go no further.

Surely the key to building new churches is not so much in the mechanics of the leadership structures, forms of worship and other external matters, important as they are, but in our co-operation with the Spirit of God who uniquely enables men and women to create and recreate something glorious for God and the salvation of men. Then we see the miracle of redemption as the halt, lame and blind become adventurers in the kingdom, discovering qualities of faith, perseverance, loyalty and love as they act in concert with God in his purpose of making all things new.

Chapter 10

Outpouring Ministries

1976

Eileen Vincent

Outpouring Ministries, originally known as the Bedmond Fellowship, was formed first in Bedmond, a rural area near St Albans. It now extends its ministry to suburban districts of Hemel Hempstead, St Albans and Watford. From an early membership of 60 in 1976 the church has grown to approximately 500 members.

While the Watford, Hemel Hempstead and St Albans churches are now autonomous, Alan Vincent is the founder and overall leader of the work. Though he has no formal theological training, he and his wife Eileen served God for many years in India, where he first developed his preaching and teaching gifts. Alan and Eileen have three children. Alan enjoys doing practical jobs on the car.

Bedmond is a small Hertfordshire village sandwiched between a tiny corrugated iron Anglican church to the north, and a pub a few hundred yards south. In the early 1960s you could have driven through, hardly noticing the village.

Fame came to Bedmond when the fields gave way to an award-winning development of council houses to resettle Londoners. The flimsy houses were as out-of-place as the

300 bewildered new residents. Their coming changed the sleepy village and uprooted the old ways as savagely as the bulldozers had torn out the hedges and trees. A new era had begun.

On the opposite side of the road to the 'tin church', as it was affectionately called, hidden away behind high privet hedges was an even smaller sombre Baptist chapel. The heavy door opened into a cold porch with barely space for three people; then a green baize door, designed to keep the warmth in, opened on to a high roofed hall with white-washed walls. The imposing shiny varnished pulpit took almost a quarter of the floor space. The congregation shunted along the wooden pews stationing themselves near to the heaters. On the back wall were ancient elongated hooks for top hats, to remind us of the days when no gentleman would be out and about without his hat.

Long before the new houses incongruously grew around the old chapel, a small handful of people met there to worship God Sunday by Sunday. Two elderly ladies continued praying and cleaned the chapel until the Sunday meetings died, with the promotion of the congregation to heaven!

Initial Growth

New things began to happen in 1958. Two or three people who loved the Lord started to attend and the doors opened again on Sundays. Children were brought in by bus for Sunday School and the antique organ squeezed out old choruses, now sung with new fervour.

In 1966 Alan, our family and I returned from India for an extended furlough. Our first period of missionary service had radically changed us. We went out as 'good evangelical Christians' and came back baptised in the Holy Spirit. Now speaking in tongues, believing in our power and authority to cast out demons in the name of Jesus, we prayed for the sick, expecting them to be healed. Trying to fit back into our local Baptist church was like putting the proverbial square peg into a round hole. Uncomfortably we squirmed for a few weeks till the Lord showed us what to do.

'Would you come and preach for us at Bedmond?' Alan was asked. 'A few new people have come in and we are reviving the old work.' Alan had previously preached once or twice to the small congregation at Bedmond before we went to India, so he was happy to accept.

We were bursting to share with others about the baptism in the Holy Spirit; surely the truth we had discovered and the life and liberty we enjoyed was not only for ourselves? Alan preached and they were insistent that he should come and lead the work, but first their questions had to be answered. Carefully he explained to the dozen or so adults how to be baptised in the Holy Spirit. Graciously God met them and a new thing began.

When is 'new' new? A new thing is what God is doing now. It is a direct expression of the present move of the Spirit. The old chapel had gone through changes that gave the appearance of newness, but really they were small revivals of the old. Suddenly a new vision, gifts and power came by the Spirit, who alone initiates a new thing. The Bedmond Fellowship began when the whole church, apart from the children, was baptised in the Holy Spirit. It was a small beginning but a vital one.

In the infancy of the charismatic movement, church government was under the microscope; the new wine did not happily fit into the old wineskins. 'Body ministry' was in fashion. 'We all have the Spirit, so we can all minister,' was the cry. In this confusion Alan loosely led the Bedmond Fellowship, fearing to 'take over'.

The congregation consisted of local people, none travelling more than four miles, but to travel into a village immediately designated us as outsiders. We were an imported congregation as far as the local residents were concerned. None of us was happy with the situation; constantly we prayed, visited and evangelised by every means, but with very little success. The original residents of Bedmond were completely uninterested. The few church-going people had their set habits and we aliens from a mile or so away were not going to change them.

The new council houses offered us a huge challenge. The loneliness of the women at home with small children, the immorality and poverty of so many lives gave us entrance. We saw no more than six to eight people saved during the 12 years we worked there and some of those fell away. The gap between their lifestyle and ours was huge and we seemed unable to bridge it. We were sadly lacking in power, although we prayed and prayed and sought to move in the Holy Spirit.

The tiny Anglican congregation continued to meet in the tin church. The new residents never darkened the door, although the local vicar also looked upon them as something of an opportunity when they first arrived.

Although our numbers were small we shared a huge vision. It never seemed incongruous to pray and expect hundreds to be saved. The prophetic gift was always very strong among us, causing the church to pray for mighty things. We talked, prayed, and longed for revival. A mighty outpouring of God's Spirit was often the theme of prayer times held at our home, when it seemed heaven was open to us.

The time came for us to return again to India. We had spent three years with the fellowship and had all learnt much. In 1969 we left the growing church with its three leaders. They were confident that the church would continue to grow and could not have anticipated the difficulties they would meet. None of them had a developed ministry in the word, although they were able men of good heart and sincere servants of God.

Numbers had grown to about 40, a few converts had been added, but the majority of new people were hungry Christians baptised in the Spirit, who were looking for a spiritual home. The life of the fellowship was like a magnet to them. The services did not follow any denominational pattern, but the congregation sought to be led at each meeting by the Holy Spirit. We were rich in spiritual gifts; weekly there were prophecies, visions, tongues and interpretation and always someone preached the word at great length.

In our absence, a pastor was invited in 1972 and the church enjoyed a new security and growth. Numbers reached about 50, and the tiny chapel began to be too small.

The handful of faithful Anglicans meeting in the tin church dwindled till the church closed and its activities were amalgamated with a larger mother church. It had come to the notice of the Church of England authorities that whilst their congregation was vanishing the chapel seemed to be experiencing a revival. The lights burned in the tiny premises many nights a week. At meeting times, the congregation's cars monopolised all the available car-parking places. To our surprise the Anglicans, guessing the fellowship was finding itself cramped, offered the use of the tin church, which was eventually purchased. The fellowship was recognised as the viable Christian witness to the village.

With the building came a legacy of certain religious functions for which we were not very suited. We did make a noble attempt for a number of years to fulfil our rôle by providing a Remembrance Day service for the few British Legion villagers who wished to make their annual visit to church. Although we owned the building the non-churchgoing residents still regarded it as their local property and would expect the 'powers that be' to provide a religious service when they required it. For the rest of the time we were no more important to them than a dry cleaner's shop when there is no dry cleaning!

Stage Two

In 1976 we returned home to Hertfordshire to stay. We had been away from the fellowship for seven years. Before we returned, stresses within the leadership had developed and the pastor had left. The leaders invited Alan back into the work again, but at first we hesitated. There were now five leaders, but they were without a common vision. One wished to follow Paul, another Apollos, another Christ! We prayed and the Lord said to Alan that he should respond to the church; he was a father to them and they were his own children. In October 1976 we again took the leadership of Bedmond Fellowship, but this time on a completely different basis.

During our time in India we had learned a lot more about church planting. We knew now that strong direction was necessary for the work so that everyone had a sense of security. The people needed to know that the church was going somewhere, and that the vision before them was also a goal to be attained. Suddenly they were thrilled that all their energies could be put to use to see their dreams come true. For too long they had been insular, concentrating on their own holiness and becoming further and further removed from the people they had once wished to see born again.

The first stage in the reconstruction was to require all the leaders to step down. It was costly but prepared the way for Alan to appoint or reappoint, in his own time, those he saw qualified for eldership. He began to teach and put a prophetic vision before the people for the kind of church which God desired. To this end he was directed to instruct the church concerning tithing and giving, not an area with which one would choose to begin especially since, as full-time leaders, we were the main beneficiaries of the giving! However embarrassing and difficult Alan found it, the Lord kept him on the subject for weeks, and told him, it was not enough to teach tithing—he was to bring the people to obedience—they were to do it.

After about six weeks the sagging congregation of around 60 (including children) were thoroughly shaken up. Some reacted sharply to the word of God, 'What's all this pressure on money? We can't afford it, we've got a mortgage!' Others turned off, thinking it quite unnecessary to go on and on about money. The ways of God are amazing; that series of teaching changed the church. When God touched their pockets he touched their hearts. In order to give freely, the people had to be thoroughly committed. One family after another made the decision to give themselves wholly to see the church grow, regardless of personal position. Giving then became a joy. From that time on we began to build.

Certain significant prophecies were delivered during this period. They empowered the people with faith and vision. God was going to bless us and cause us to grow. Growth always means change, and change unsettles. Some became restless, wondering if they liked the new direction the church was taking. The song books were changed: the pews gave way to chairs—a major catastrophe to some, but with the departure of the formal pews, went the end of an introspective small-minded church.

How lovingly the Lord spoke to us in our situation. The prophetic word came week by week, directing and confirming our way, encouraging all to hold fast. As the church was being brought together to accomplish God's purpose, there was immediate conflict. The forces of darkness did not like it and by any means they tried to disrupt, bringing disunity and discouragement, but we were not ignorant of the devil's devices.

One Sunday morning during this shaky time of reorganisation the Lord powerfully spoke to us using the analogy of an army. He said that, as in the army, we all had a function to fulfil according to our rank. We were warned to keep rank and not to leave the camp; we were to stay regardless of difficulties. The dust of warfare settled and we came out the other side wiser. That prophetic word continued to be a steadying influence in many lives for months.

As soon as Alan began teaching and directing the church our numbers soared, mainly by the addition of families between the ages of 20 and 35. As a result we had dozens of young children. People moved into the district, hungry Christians found us, and the occasional convert thrilled us. Although we were still only a village congregation the Lord continued to speak of big things. Another prophecy told us we would plant a living church in each of the three towns about us. Bedmond village was positioned like the hub of a wheel, which encompassed Watford, St Albans and Hemel Hempstead, each about six miles from the church. The prophecy said our growth would be like that of a strawberry plant. We would send out a runner to plant a new church. Its support and life would come from Bedmond till it was established and rooted.

An expanding ministry

Our first 'strawberry plant' was the thrilling move to Garston in Watford. On Sunday mornings the tin church in 1979 was crammed full. By juggling the chair arrangements we were able to seat 153 people. Latecomers had to stand. In three years we had grown from about 30 adults to this encouraging number. Very few were from the village; a group of village boys began to attend and some were saved through the young peoples' work that continued every Friday night in the old chapel. Despite fantastic love, personal care and teaching, these boys did not remain, although some were baptised. The environment of crime and rebellion had a powerful pull upon them.

About 35 adults travelled to Bedmond from the Watford area. When the United Reformed Church building in Garston, a district of Watford, came on the property market it seemed the ideal location to start a new church. It was on the main road and adjacent to extensive 'middle class' housing and a council estate. The asking price was £70,000 but as we prayed God led us after prayer to offer £40,000 and to pay cash! We had no more than 80 wage-earners among us, but rose to the challenge. The whole church was involved in this venture. It was the fulfilment of prophecy. We knew that the Lord was with us.

After everyone had given all they had, we were still £16,000 short. With only a few days from completion, we decided to take an offering in faith. The little baskets handed around the cramped tin church miraculously yielded £16,000! Our target was reached and the roof nearly lifted with praises. In February 1980 we purchased the building for God's price.

God had provided for the leadership of the new work by adding David and Daphne Barker to the fellowship in November 1975, when they were recent converts. It was obvious God was calling David, and he proved himself to be fit for leadership. The plan was that Alan and myself with David and the local Watford people should relocate in Garston and start again.

The remaining two elders continued to guide the work at Bedmond and Alan preached there occasionally. Through united meetings at Garston on Sunday evenings, as well as joint prayer meetings, teaching sessions and women's meetings, the churches remained as one under Alan's ministry. The eldership of both churches continued to meet together and pooled all their resources including finance.

Growth in the new locality

At first we looked a pitiful group, 27 adults plus children in the huge building seating about 250; but almost immediately the Garston church, as it is called, began to grow. The empty seats seemed to invite people.

To our surprise our presence posed a threat to other

churches in the area. There were those who accused us of 'sheep-stealing', but in fact we never went out of our way to attract anyone from any other church. We were concerned to minister to those God had given us and fulfil the vision we had received. The presence of God in our meetings, enthusiastic worship and praise and the excellent ministry of the word attracted starved Christians who were fed and brought on to maturity. Gifts and ministries were being developed and again, rich prophecy encouraged us to believe for the most incredible big things at a time when our voices echoed in the almost empty hall.

The Sunday morning service lasted about two hours and was an unstructured occasion when above all we wished to be guided by the Holy Spirit. Usually there was a time of free worship with the ministry of gifts of the Spirit. In those days it was mainly prophecy and sometimes tongues with interpretation. Songs in the Spirit with heavenly themes were given to some, and we prayed for the sick. Usually this time culminated in breaking of bread which was shared by all, including the children.

As the congregation was mainly young married couples, during the preaching we had a good Sunday School and a crèche for the babies. Every Sunday was a feast in God's word. We were bountifully blessed; anyone looking for a short sermon in Garston Church had come to the wrong place! The ministry of the word usually lasted an hour.

Sunday evenings followed a different pattern. Alan often took a series which would continue for months. These occasions attracted many visitors, and some eventually joined the church. A recurring activity on Sunday evenings was baptising the stream of new people from both Bedmond and Garston churches, which were both growing. At first they were mainly relocated Christians, or lapsed believers who had repented, but after a year or so it changed. There was great joy one night when the majority of those being baptised by immersion had brand new testimonies of salvation. Those Sunday evenings were special—with fantastic exuberance. God was blessing us; the building that had seemed so huge was now crammed full and people had to go home to make room for the visitors.

We had reached the next stage in our development. David Barker was now full-time in the ministry and Alan Stevens was appointed as a second elder in the Garston Church.

One memorable Sunday evening, God told Alan to ask for an army of 10,000; ten thousand people committed and ready to work. God planted that impossible goal in our hearts; but because it was so big, no definite steps were taken to bring it about. In August 1981 we went to Seoul, Korea. Alan wanted to see the largest church in the world, and we were deeply challenged by what we saw. We returned sure, however, that the strawberry plant method of growth was for us.

In Yonggi Cho's church in Seoul, we had discovered that cell groups were the spearhead for growth. We had established housegroups in the churches, but their emphasis was pastoral and teaching. Somehow we never seemed able to steer our housegroups away from that emphasis, and up to this day we have not successfully used them for evangelism.

Continued expansion

Again we were ready to plant another church. Twenty-seven adults living in St Albans who travelled either to Garston or Bedmond were pressing to begin a new church in St Albans. Peter Byers, one of the elders from Bedmond, took the group, who rented a school hall for Sundays. Maple church was born and within a year had grown to over 100. They walked into a spiritual vacuum where dozens of dissatisfied Spirit-filled believers, mainly Anglicans, were longing for a church where they could grow in the Spirit. Maple church soon outgrew the small hall and moved into another school. Three years later, they number 200 and continue to grow.

Alan now stretched himself between the three churches. Whilst St Albans and Garston continued to grow as individual churches; the elders of all three churches continued to meet weekly. Alan was accepted as the leader and inspiration behind each church. The ties of friendship between the people brought us willingly together but as each church grew, it became increasingly difficult to find a hall large enough, in which to meet.

About the same time Garston Church also sent out about 40 to 50 people to found a church in Stanmore. A group had transferred to Garston from a Baptist church there, about a year earlier. They met in housegroups in their own locality until they found a building. Once the move was made, others joined them and they soon grew to fill their little building. The Stanmore church, now numbering over 130, does not keep the same close contact as the other churches founded.

The remaining congregation at Bedmond, now left with only one elder; not a full-time man, became static. Two groups had gone out from them including leaders and promising ministries. They were in need of vision and a new challenge. For some time we had been considering starting a day school. Fortuitously a redundant school became available for rent which wonderfully provided for the children's needs as well as a home for a new church. The move out of the village into Hemel Hempstead was a joyous occasion—the fulfilment of prophecy.

Suddenly the church had new life, as if it had received a blood transfusion. The people were excited and thrilled at the possibility of growth and challenged by the new environment. Bourne Valley Community Church began with about 60 people, but immediately grew. At first most of the addition was families from our other churches who moved into Hemel Hempstead for the school. That means of growth continues. Another man joined the eldership, and the pastor became full-time. Steadily as he matures in his ministry and in faith, the work grows and has given no sign of reaching a plateau. In three years they have gathered approximately 250 people.

With the introduction of housegroups in 1977, a commitment course was started. Every person in each church has passed through this basic teaching, which identifies the standards which the church expects of those who are committed members. Commitment to prayer, evangelism, giving, corporate worship and submission to those set over us in the Lord, changed the church from a loose gathering of those pleasing themselves to an army with a common purpose. When we gather for prayer the whole church is involved; when we are reaching out in faith for new premises we all share the burden. We are united to bring about God's purpose for us.

From the beginning we have always had a lively women's work, with good teaching and opportunity to meet the pastoral needs of the women. A number have been converted, baptised in the Spirit and drawn into the life of the church through these meetings.

Now there are a variety of separate meetings. Women's coffee and chat is a great opportunity for counsel and prayer as well as straight teaching times or prayer meetings. The young people have their own programme as well as a 17-plus group, a football team (now top of the local league), keep-fit group, and many others.

Since an evangelist, Steve Maile, has joined the staff of the churches our methods of evangelism have changed. We had been periodically going *en masse*, mums and babies as well, to sing, praise the Lord and talk to people on the High Street. This yielded a little fruit, but Steve is now training groups to become involved in pub and door-to-door work, as well as street evangelism. A concentrated training school in evangelism is planned for 1986, through which we hope to form permanent groups for evangelism.

Steve has countless openings into schools in a wide area

and is seeing numbers of young people saved. The major problem is getting them established in the churches. We have new believers' classes running continuously; every effort is made to gather those who are saved, but we are constantly aware of the enemy's attacks.

The most important factor in planting a new church and in its growth is the quality of the pastor. If he has faith, is called and appointed by God, and moves in his God-given ministry, a church will grow. It will be unique, because we all differ. The pastor or leader must then have other able men with a vocation to join him in the leadership: only as the leadership grows can the church grow. Leaders differ in their level of ability and measure of faith; therefore all churches do not have the same potential for size.

I was privileged to be present at the Church Growth International meetings held by Yonggi Cho in Oslo in 1983. There I saw Ben Crandall, a pastor of a large church in New York, demonstrate the crucial need for expanding church leadership. He said, pointing to the table in front of him, 'If I was to tip sand upon this table there would come a point when it would pour off the edges. No matter how much I prayed, pleaded with God or commanded, if I kept pouring the sand, it would continue to fall on the floor. What do I need? I need a bigger table if I am going to support more sand. I need a bigger leadership if I am to support more people.' Ben Crandall used this to illustrate the essential part played in his church by housegroups and their leaders.

We are now at a stage in our development where again we need a new challenge. It seems that if a work is to continue to grow rather than to 'consolidate' (a word not found in my Bible!) the people need to be progressively taken forward from goal to goal. Once a target is attained—a building filled, new housegroups established—it is time to move on, time to present the next challenge. Too easily we stand still and pat ourselves on the back; before long we are losing ground.

God has brought us back again to his impossible invitation—an army of 10,000! For years Alan has tried to see this come about by inspiring the leaders of our churches but recently the Lord said to him—'I told you to build a large church. I promised you an army of 10,000.' Painstakingly Alan has retraced his steps and has again taken up the reins of direct leadership in Garston Church were we believe God intends to build a significant work.

Once again, on Sundays it is hard to find a seat so we are negotiating for a very large local premises which gives scope for 10,000. By faith we go ahead.

One of the promises God gave was an adequate supply of men, finance and buildings to do his will. Again we are claiming them, but this time on a far larger scale. Like a seed, Garston Church is sown into the inviting soil of faith, and we expect to grow something glorious to the praise of Jesus.